SMARTY JONES RELAXES
AT HOME IN BENSALEM'S
PHILADELPHIA PARK.
AP/WWP

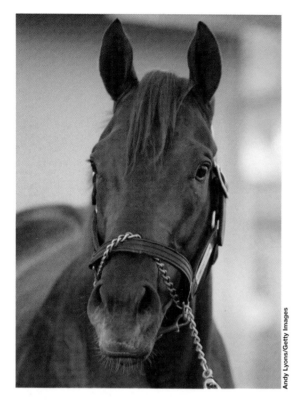

Andy Lyons/Getty Images

SMARTY JONES WINS AQUEDUCT FEATURE

January 3, 2004

NEW YORK (AP)—Smarty Jones won the $81,225 Count Fleet Stakes at Aqueduct on Saturday, scoring a five-length victory to remain undefeated in three career starts.

Smarty Jones, the favorite ridden by Stewart Elliott and carrying 116 pounds, took the lead near the middle of the stretch.

Risky Trick was second in the field of seven 3-year-olds. Mr. Spock was another six lengths back in third.

The winner covered the mile and 70 yards in 1:41 2-5 over a fast track to earn $48,735 for Someday Farm.

Smarty Jones returned $2.80, $2.70 and $2.30. Risky Trick paid $10.60 and $4.40 and Mr. Spock showed.

SMARTY JONES

America's Horse

www.SportsPublishingllc.com

Publisher: Peter L. Bannon
Senior Managing Editor: Susan M. Moyer
Photo Editor: Erin Linden-Levy
Book Design: InnerWorkings, LLC.
Cover Design: Dustin Hubbart

Front Cover Image: Doug Pensinger/Getty Images
Back Cover Image: AP/WWP

ISBN: 1-58261-912-3

Printed in the United States.

Sports Publishing LLC
www.SportsPublishingLLC.com

CONTENTS

*"America loves a folk hero.
Even if it's temporary.
Even if it's a horse.
Especially if it's a horse."*

FAN QUOTE

SMARTY FACTS

Smarty Jones was not his original name. Pat Chapman submitted the name "Get Along" when registering the foal. She then changed it to the nickname of her own mother, who shared the same birthday as Smarty, February 28. Chapman had to pay $100 to get the name changed.

Smarty's winning Preakness time of 1:55.59 was faster than the winning time posted by Funny Cide (1:55.61), Red Bullet (1:56.04), Tabasco Cat (1:56.25) or War Emblem (1:56.63).

Smarty is just more than 15 hands high. Rock Hard Ten is 17 hands high.

At 1:45 p.m. Preakness Day, Smarty's odds were 1-5.

The back of Servis' Smarty Jones cap reads: "We're Jonesin'"

When Smarty's dam, I'll Get Along, was bred to Elusive Quality, stud fee was $10,000. The Chapmans paid $40,000 for I'll Get Along. Investment: $50,000. Return: $7.3 million. So far.

According to the *Philadelphia Inquirer*, a man registered the Web address smartyjones.com and posted the domain on EBay with a "buy it now" price of $139,500. This was before the Preakness.

MARIO ARRIAGAS DRIES
SMARTY JONES AFTER A BATH.

"I'm so shaken. It's just a gift from God."

TRAINER JOHN SERVIS' WIFE SHERRY

SMARTY JONES WINS SOUTHWEST STAKES

February 29, 2004

HOT SPRINGS, ARK. (AP)—Smarty Jones won the $100,000 Southwest Stakes for 3-year-olds at Oaklawn Park on Saturday, his fourth straight win and second stakes victory.

Jockey Stewart Elliot, who tops the standings at the current Philadelphia Park meet, was at Oaklawn for the first time to ride Smarty Jones to victory. Smarty Jones paid $3, $3 and $2.20.

Two Down Automatic finished second and returned $4.40 and $2.20. Pro Prado paid $2.20 to show.

Trained by John Servis, Smarty Jones made his first start since winning the Count Fleet at Aqueduct on January 3. The one-mile Southwest is a prep race for the Rebel Stakes on March 20 and the Arkansas Derby.

OWNER PATRICIA CHAPMAN LEADS SMARTY JONES AND JOCKEY STEWART ELLIOTT TO THE OAKLAWN PARK WINNER'S CIRCLE.
AP/WWP

"*I am very pleased with Smarty's move. I wanted him to finish up strong, and he did.*"

TRAINER JOHN SERVIS

SMARTY JONES AND JOCKEY STEWART ELLIOTT
FINISH AHEAD OF TWO DOWN AUTOMATIC TO
WIN THE SOUTHWEST STAKES. AP/WWP

JOCKEY STEWART ELLIOTT AND SMARTY JONES RACE TO REBEL STAKES VICTORY, THEIR FIFTH WIN IN FIVE STARTS.

AP/WWP

"Awesome. He's a running machine."

SMARTY JONES BARN FOREMAN BILL FOSTER

SMARTY JONES WINS THIRD STRAIGHT STAKES RACE AT REBEL

DOUGLAS PILS

March 21, 2004

HOT SPRINGS, ARK (AP)—Smarty Jones won his fifth race in five starts and his third straight stakes race, running away with the $200,000 Rebel Stakes for 3-year-olds on Saturday at Oaklawn Park.

Winner of the Southwest Stakes here last month and the Count Fleet at Aqueduct on January 3, Smarty Jones broke with trainer Todd Pletcher's Purge in the 1 1-16-mile race.

Purge, a winner in two starts at six furlongs, led until jockey Stewart Elliott spurred Smarty Jones into the lead coming into the stretch and winning by 3¼ lengths over the nine-horse field.

The victory put Smarty Jones in line for Oaklawn's $5 million Centennial Bonus should he also win the Arkansas Derby on April 10 and the Kentucky Derby on May 1. Oaklawn instituted the bonus to mark its 100th anniversary.

Trained by John Servis, Smarty Jones is the one horse that lived up to expectations in Saturday's three Kentucky Derby prep races.

Smarty Jones paid $9, $4.60 and $3.40 and Purge returned $4.50 and $3.80. Pro Prado, trained by Bob Holthus and ridden by John McKee, finished third and paid $3.60.

The Rebel is the last major prep race at Oaklawn before the Arkansas Derby.

GROOMSMAN MARIO ARRIAGAS GUIDES SMARTY JONES TO THE WINNER'S CIRCLE.
AP/WWP

SMARTY JONES WINS ARKANSAS DERBY

DOUGLAS PILS

April 11, 2004

HOT SPRINGS, ARK. (AP)—A horse from Pennsylvania is on his way to Churchill Downs for the Kentucky Derby.

Smarty Jones remained undefeated in six races, stalking Purge just as he had last month in the Rebel and charging past him on the turn to win the $1 million Arkansas Derby at Oaklawn Park.

The victory Saturday gives Philadelphia-based trainer John Servis and jockey Stewart Elliott their first trip to the Kentucky Derby on May 1. At Churchill, Smarty Jones will attempt to become the first undefeated Derby winner since Seattle Slew in 1977.

"I'm very fortunate to be in Philadelphia Park and to have the clients I have," Servis said. "I have good owners that give me the opportunity to get a hold of horses like this. When you get horses like this, it makes it real easy to get up in the morning."

Borrego finished second, 1¹/₂ lengths behind Smarty Jones, while Pro Prado charged from seventh to third in front of 62,264 fans.

Smarty Jones ran 1 1-8 miles in 1:49.41. Breaking from the outside post, Smarty Jones met Purge, who started from the No. 5 position, as they entered the first turn. They hit the first quarter in 22.64 seconds on the muddy track, and finished a half-mile at 46.95.

SMARTY JONES OUTPACES BORREGO (LEFT)
AND THE REST OF THE FIELD DOWN THE
STRETCH TO WIN THE ARKANSAS DERBY.
AP/WWP

"I let him get running a little bit and then Purge got going a bit and it set up from there," Elliott said. "I thought we were clipping along pretty good, but he's a fast horse."

The win also puts Smarty Jones, the derby's even-money favorite, in line for Oaklawn's "Centennial Bonus" if he can win the Kentucky Derby. The bonus was instituted this year to commemorate the track's 100th birthday and the first two legs of the bonus were the Rebel and the Arkansas Derby.

The $5 million bonus, half of which will come out of Oaklawn owner Charles Cella's pocket, matches what Visa has offered for a potential Triple Crown winner since 1995.

The only horse to win the Rebel, Arkansas and Kentucky Derbys was Sunny's Halo in 1983.

Combined with the $800,000 Smarty Jones would get for winning the Kentucky Derby, the $5.8 million payday would be the richest in horse racing history. This for a horse who didn't have any graded stakes earnings before Saturday.

"Today, for me, was the pressure race," Servis said. "This was it, because he if he didn't win today he wasn't going to go."

Smarty Jones would join Lil E. Tee (1992) as the only Pennsylvania-bred horses to win at Kentucky. Last year, Funny Cide became the first New York-bred horse to win at Kentucky.

Smarty Jones was the only favorite to follow through with a victory in the three Kentucky Derby prep races Saturday. In the other two, Tapit beat favored Master David in the Wood Memorial at Aqueduct and The Cliff's Edge ran down Lion Heart in the Blue Grass Stakes at Kenneland.

Smarty Jones, who ran the last eighth in 12.5 seconds, earned $600,000 for the Chapmans in winning the Grade 2 race. He has $878,355 in career earnings, but the win gives him the first graded stakes earnings of his career.

"I can't tell you how good this makes me feel," said Roy Chapman, who is battling emphysema and wasn't able to travel for the Rebel on March 20. "It's unbelievable to see the way that horse ran today."

PURGE (5), RIDDEN BY CORNELIO VELAZQUEZ, LEADS SMARTY JONES INTO THE FIRST TURN OF THE ARKANSAS DERBY.
AP/WWP

SMARTY JONES KICKS UP
HIS HEELS DURING
A WORKOUT AT
PHILADELPHIA PARK.
AP/WWP

SMARTY JONES WORKS OUT IN PREPARATION FOR THE KENTUCKY DERBY AT CHURCHILL DOWNS IN LOUISVILLE.

Matthew Stockman/Getty Images

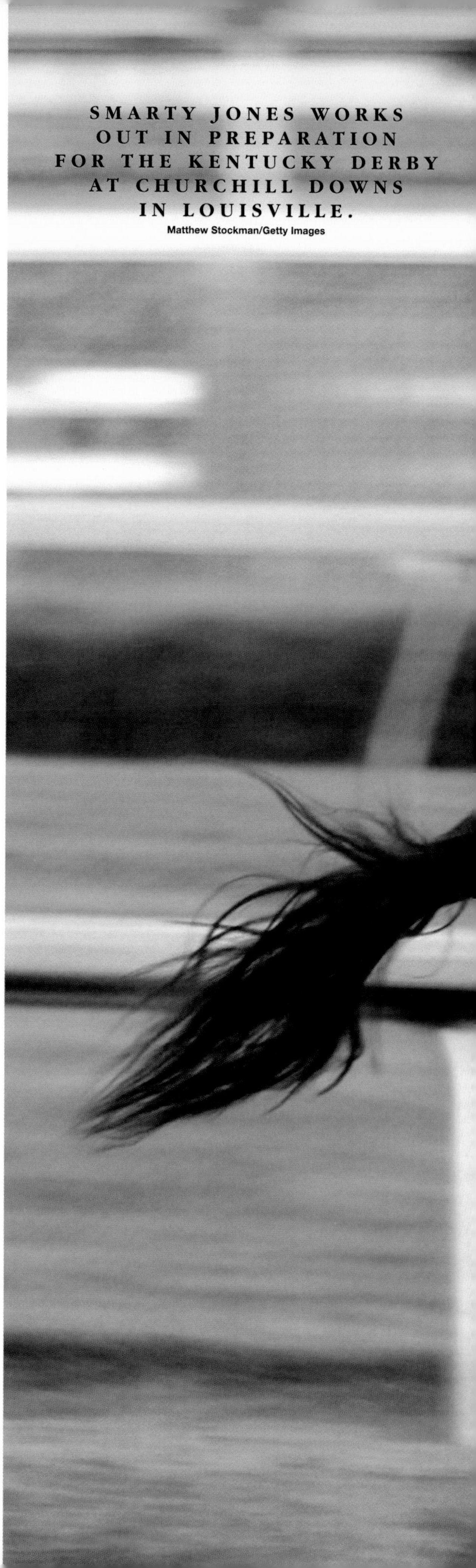

SMARTY JONES A WINNER EVEN BEFORE THE DERBY

RICHARD ROSENBLATT

April 25, 2004

CLARKSBURG, N.J. (AP)—Dr. Patricia Hogan shook her head as she looked at the thoroughbred's X-ray. Where there should have been a solid expanse of bone around the horse's eye was instead a crazed swath of lines and shadows, as if someone had taken a hammer to it.

The 2-year-old racehorse had reared up and smashed his head on an iron bar at Philadelphia Park, fracturing his skull and driving his eye deep into his head.

"When he got here the whole left side of his head was just a balloon," Hogan recalled last week. Where the eye had been, there was only tissue.

But the accident was only a detour in the improbable journey of the undefeated Smarty Jones, a journey that began with a murdered trainer and could end up in the winner's circle at Churchill Downs following Saturday's Kentucky Derby.

"To be part of this story is just unbelievable," said Pat Chapman, who owns Smarty Jones with her husband, Roy. "Let's just say we've been very lucky the way things have turned out."

On February 28, 2001, a wine-colored colt was born on the Chapmans' farm in Chester County, Pennsylvania.

The horse was named for Pat Chapman's mother, Mildred Jones, who was nicknamed "Smarty" and shared the colt's February 28 birthday. All was well, and the Chapmans were hoping for that rare combination of speed and stamina from their latest homebred.

"Good horses like that always look like they're going slower than they are, but when you put a watch on them, they take your breath away."

FARM MANAGER GEORGE ISAACS

Before the year was out, however, the Chapmans' world turned upside down.

In early December, their longtime trainer, 60-year-old Bobby Camac, and his wife were found shot and killed at their New Jersey home. Camac's stepson was charged with murder.

"It was a total shock, numbing," Chapman said. "We didn't know what to do next."

The Chapmans were so distraught, they all but got out of the horse business. They disbanded their breeding operation and got rid of all their horses except two—a slow 2-year-old and Smarty Jones.

Realizing they weren't ready to call it quits, Smarty Jones was sent in 2002 to Bridlewood Farm in Ocala, Florida, to prepare for racing. It didn't take long for the yearling to make an impression on farm manager George Isaacs.

"He kind of moved like Michael Jordan in a bridle, smooth as silk," Isaacs said. "Good horses like that always look like they're going slower than they are, but when you put a watch on them they take your breath away."

On July 16, 2003, Smarty Jones' Florida vacation was over, and he was sent to Philadelphia Park. His new trainer would be John Servis.

Just 12 days into training, misfortune struck again.

While schooling in the starting gate on July 28, the colt suddenly reared up and slammed his head on an unpadded iron bar. Blood gushed out of his nostrils, and Servis thought Smarty Jones was dead.

"All four of his legs were buckled underneath him like he was going to lay down, and his head was actually underneath him between his legs," Servis said. "And he was out cold."

At the New Jersey Equine Clinic, an ultrasound found Smarty's left eye to be intact, though it wasn't until the swelling subsided three days later that Hogan knew Smarty Jones hadn't lost any vision.

Smarty Jones was a model patient. They wrapped his head in thick cushioned bandages and called him Quasimodo. Through it all, Smarty never sulked. "He'd stand in his stall hollering at the other horses, and he'd never miss a meal," Hogan said.

By August 8, Smarty Jones was discharged to spend the next month grazing on a farm. When he finally returned to the track, Servis brought him along slowly: A walk to the track one time, a rider on his back another, an accompanying pony the next time out.

Finally, it was time to face a starting gate.

"It took about two weeks before he was comfortable, but to this day he'll step back a little," said Servis. "It was a pretty serious injury, but he's learned to handle it."

Perfectly, so far. The feisty Smarty Jones, who stands a smallish 15.3 hands—"with a big heart," says Pat Chapman—is 6-for-6 and has a chance to become the first unbeaten Derby winner since Seattle Slew in 1977.

Not bad for a horse who is trained by a small-track trainer and ridden by a small-track jockey in Stewart Elliott, both preparing for their first Derby.

After Smarty's first win at Philly Park on November 9, Servis knew he had a talented horse, "but I had no idea how talented."

More victories followed, but Smarty Jones still hadn't run in a graded stake. And if more than the maximum of 20 horses entered the Derby, graded-stakes money would determine the field.

In April, he won the $1 million Arkansas Derby, a Grade 2 event. That victory puts him in line to collect a $5 million "Centennial Bonus" offered by Oaklawn Park for a sweep of the Rebel, Arkansas Derby and Kentucky Derby.

"Everyone here is rooting for him," said Hogan, who plans to have a Derby day Smarty party featuring Smarty Jones caps.

After the first win, the clinic staff started a bulletin board for Smarty, and they've been adding news clippings and photos ever since. Above one of the pictures showing Smarty Jones in the winner's circle, someone added their own caption: "Look at Quasimodo now!"

**SMARTY JONES GETS A BATH
AFTER HIS PRACTICE RUN.**

"He kind of moved like Michael Jordan in a bridle, smooth as silk." FARM MANAGER GEORGE ISAACS

A TALE NEARLY AS OLD AS HORSE RACING ITSELF

JIM LITKE

April 29, 2004

LOUISVILLE, KY. (AP)—In some ways, this place has never felt so unfamiliar.

Glance at the grandstand and everything looks as if it's under construction, except for the fabled Twin Spires.

So maybe it's only fitting, with the ancient dowager Churchill Downs halfway through a $121 million facelift, that the most captivating story at the Kentucky Derby is nearly as old as horse racing itself.

The star of the tale is an undersized chestnut named Smarty Jones, whose difficulties could fill two barns. Barely nine months ago, before his first race, Smarty's handlers were training him in the starting gate when the horse suddenly reared, struck his head on an iron bar and knocked himself cold.

"Oh, my God," trainer John Servis yelped as the colt lay unconscious on the dirt. "The horse killed himself."

Not quite—though Smarty did put a sizable dent in his skull, not to mention the dreams of a half-dozen people whose decades in racing were filled with as many tragedies as triumphs, but not even one horse good enough to get them to the Derby.

"If you haven't been here yet, after all this time, you start to think, 'What are your chances now?'" jockey Stewart Elliott said.

The morning sun glinted off his shiny black leather riding vest and bathed the front of Smarty Jones' stall in a soft white glow. Elliott has won more than 3,200 races up and down the Atlantic seaboard, but not one you've ever heard of.

Last year, he watched the Derby at home on TV as Funny Cide began an improbable run of his own.

Now, the horse that will put Elliott squarely in the middle of that same picture was standing just off his right shoulder, idly pulling clumps of hay from a bale nailed to the wall.

"It just goes to show," Elliott said, "that in this business, you never know."

That could be the motto for the strivers and unknowns who hitched their star to a gritty Pennsylvania-bred. They watched him win race after race—six in all without a defeat—all the way to the starting gate at Churchill Downs as the 9-2 second-choice on the first Saturday in May.

His owners, Roy and Pat Chapman, a car dealer and former social worker, didn't get into the racket until late in life, and even then, only as a sidelight. They bought 100 acres outside Philadelphia and started making plans that never seemed to go anywhere.

"Every day we'd get up and say, 'someday we're going

SMARTY JONES SIZES UP
THE COMPETITION AT
CHURCHILL DOWNS.

Andy Lyons/Getty Images

AP/WWP

to do this, someday we're going to do that,'" Pat Chapman recalled, "and so we wound up calling it Someday Farm."

Roy Chapman, hooked up to an oxygen tank and sitting nearby in a wheelchair, chuckled at the memory. He has emphysema and struggles to speak sometimes, but for the moment his life couldn't be much easier.

His family was gathered around him and Servis' 10-year-old son, Tyler, stood behind him, gently massaging Chapman's shoulders.

He doesn't have the time or the breath to tell the story of how Smarty Jones wound up in his barn, but the short version is this:

The Chapmans hired a trainer named Bob Camac, who found the dam and stallion that sired Smarty Jones. Nine months later, Camac was found shot to death in his New Jersey home.

Because of Roy's health, the Chapmans had already begun curtailing their modest racing operation; Camac's death nearly drove them out of the business altogether.

After selling most of their stock, they sent Smarty Jones to Florida to be broken. "He kind of moved like Michael Jordan in a bridle, smooth as silk," said George Isaacs, the horseman who handled those chores.

At Isaacs' urging, the Chapmans kept Smarty and sent him to Servis instead.

Like Elliott, Servis was a regular winner at Philadelphia Park but largely unknown outside that corner of the racing world. The two of them hooked up in 1980, at the start of what would become a very successful partnership.

But the closer they came to breaking into the big time, the more they must have wondered whether they'd both be around for the end of the ride. After all, the last time Derby rookies combined to win the race was 25 years ago.

So someone asked Roy Chapman whether he ever considered replacing Servis.

"I think we talked about it exactly once. He said, 'You know, Roy, this is a special horse.' And I said, 'Then it's up to you to get me to the Derby,'" Chapman said.

Chapman didn't even bother discussing the matter with Elliott.

"No way," Chapman said. "He's Mr. Cool. And he's already shown he knows how to ride this horse."

And a few minutes later, Chapman steered his chair slowly across the bumpy lawn outside Smarty Jones' barn toward a car.

Off in the distance, beyond the storied oval racetrack, the sun reflected off the hundreds of new panes of glass lining the renovated clubhouse, shining like a giant beacon.

But if you lowered your gaze and kept it fixed on the finish line for a moment, Churchill Downs looked much the same as it always does: like gold at the end of a sporting rainbow.

STEWART ELLIOTT FIELDS
QUESTIONS FROM THE MEDIA
BEFORE THE KENTUCKY
DERBY.
Matthew Stockman/Getty Images

SMARTY JONES AND HIS JOCKEY CROSS THE FINISH LINE TO WIN THE 130TH KENTUCKY DERBY.
Matthew Stockman/Getty Images

Jeff Haynes/AFP/Getty Images

SMARTY JONES WINS KENTUCKY DERBY

RICHARD ROSENBLATT

May 2, 2004

LOUISVILLE, KY. (AP)—Here we go again.

A nice but hardly heralded horse wins the Kentucky Derby. That's what happened last year with Funny Cide, and it happened again Saturday with Smarty Jones.

Splashing his way past Lion Heart in the stretch, the 3-year-old chestnut colt won America's premier horse race and is well on his way to winning racing fans' hearts.

"He seems to be the people's horse," Derby rookie rider Stewart Elliott said, echoing the sentiments of those who watched Funny Cide go for the Triple Crown last year.

The victory triggered the biggest payday in the sport, with the undefeated favorite earning a $5 million bonus from Oaklawn Park along with the Derby winner's share of $854,800.

QUINTONS GOLD RUSH, RIDDEN BY COREY NAKATANI, POLLARD'S VISION, RIDDEN BY JOHN VELAZQUEZ AND SMARTY JONES HEAD DOWN THE FRONT STRETCH AT CHURCHILL DOWNS.
Matthew Stockman/Getty Images)

SMARTY JONES PULLS
AWAY FROM THE PACK
AND SPRINTS FOR
THE FINISH LINE.
Matthew Stockman/Getty Images

Smarty Jones ran his record to 7-for-7 and became the first unbeaten Derby winner since Seattle Slew in 1977. Seattle Slew went on to win the Triple Crown, a feat Smarty Jones will attempt when he heads to the Preakness in two weeks.

"I don't think this horse has ever got the respect he was due," 77-year-old owner Roy Chapman said.

Probably because his story is a doozy.

Smarty is a Pennsylvania-bred who nearly died when he slammed his head on an iron bar; his trainer and jockey are based at a small-time park; his owners refused a blank check to sell him.

He doesn't have the regal bearing of a champion. He's smallish and has goofy bangs that brush the top of his eyes. But nothing has stopped him so far.

Even over a sloppy track at Churchill Downs— the first in 10 years—Smarty Jones raced just behind pace-setter Lion Heart. As the 18-horse field came off the final turn, the colt moved up to challenge for the lead. Under Elliott, Smarty Jones staged his patented stretch surge with an eighth of a mile to go and pulled away.

He won by 2 3/4 lengths over Lion Heart, with Imperialism, trained by 21-year-old Kristin Mulhall, third.

"At the three-eighths pole I was biding my time," Elliott said. "I knew I had a loaded gun beneath me. He straightened up, switched leads and I figured it was time to go.

"When I had the chance, I took it. I was pretty confident when we passed Lion Heart," he said.

The winning time for the 1¼-mile Derby was a slow 2:04.06 over the fourth sloppy track in Derby history. Though it didn't rain during the race, there was a downpour two hours earlier that left the track a muddy mess and filled the infield with small lakes.

That his first Derby was raced over slop hardly mattered to winning trainer John Servis: "That was a beautiful race. Picture perfect."

Mike Smith, aboard Lion Heart, concurred: "I had a great trip, but Smarty Jones just had another gear."

Servis and Elliott, a pair of Philadelphia Park regulars, became the first trainer-jockey duo to win the Derby on their first try since favorite Spectacular Bid won in 1979 for trainer Bud Delp and jockey Rodney Franklin.

THE CROWD ROARS IN THE BACKGROUND AS SMARTY JONES WINS THE 130TH KENTUCKY DERBY.

Andy Lyons/Getty Images

"I had a great trip and had every opportunity to beat him, but Smarty Jones just had another gear today…I tried to get away from him and he hung with me, so I knew it was going to be a dogfight to the end. Everything worked to a "T", but I didn't win."

JOCKEY OF LION HEART MIKE SMITH

STEWART ELLIOTT GUIDES SMARTY JONES TO THE FINISH AND THE WINNER'S CIRCLE.
Andy Lyons/Getty Images

"I knew I had a loaded gun beneath me. He straightened up, switched leads and I figured it was time to go."

JOCKEY STEWART ELLIOT

And even though the favorite won, until the gates opened, the race was considered a wide-open affair with at least a half dozen horses capable of winning, including Blue Grass Stakes winner The Cliff's Edge and Wood Memorial winner Imperialism.

In the stands, Chapman got out of his wheelchair and shouted, "I can't believe it!" and accepted hugs from Servis, friends and relatives. Chapman, hooked up to an oxygen tank because of his emphysema, then sat back down, taking deep breaths to calm himself, but smiling the whole time.

"We've never raced at this level," said Chapman, a retired auto dealer who got into the horse business in the mid 1980s. "Never thought we would get here until we met Smarty. And this guy sitting next to me." He pointed to Servis.

Chapman and his wife, Pat, will now collect a $5 million bonus from Oaklawn Park in Hot Springs, Arkansas, because their horse swept the Rebel Stakes, Arkansas Derby and Kentucky Derby. With the huge payoff, Smarty Jones becomes racing's sixth richest horse with earnings of $6,733,155.

The 4-1 favorite paid $10.20, $6.20 and $4.80 in becoming just the fifth undefeated Derby winner. Lion Heart paid $8.20 and $5.80. Imperialism returned $6.20 to show. Limehouse was fourth, followed by The Cliff's Edge, Action This Day, Read the Footnotes, Birdstone, Tapit, Borrego, Song of the Sword, Master David, Pro Prado, Castledale, Friends Lake, Minister Eric and Pollard's Vision. Quintons Gold Rush did not finish.

The crowd, 140,054, was the smallest since 1994, when Go for Gin won over the last sloppy track.

Last year, Funny Cide became the first New York-bred to win the Derby. Smarty Jones becomes just the second Pennsylvania-bred—Lil E. Tee in 1992 was the first. Funny Cide also had a first-time Derby trainer and owners, but any other similarities end there.

Smarty Jones finally made it to the races, and hasn't stopped running since. He broke his maiden on November 9, winning by $7^3/4$ lengths at Philly Park. He won by 15 lengths two weeks later—and that's when Servis knew he had himself a Derby horse.

Then it was on to New York, where he won the Count Fleet at Aqueduct before Servis took him to Arkansas. Smarty Jones then won the Southwest Stakes and Rebel Stakes, but still hadn't earned any graded stakes money, something that was needed to make the Derby field.

A win in the Grade 2 Arkansas Derby was crucial, and Smarty came through—in the rain. He blew past Borrego and won by $1^1/2$ lengths and it was on to Churchill Downs.

And now it's on to Baltimore.

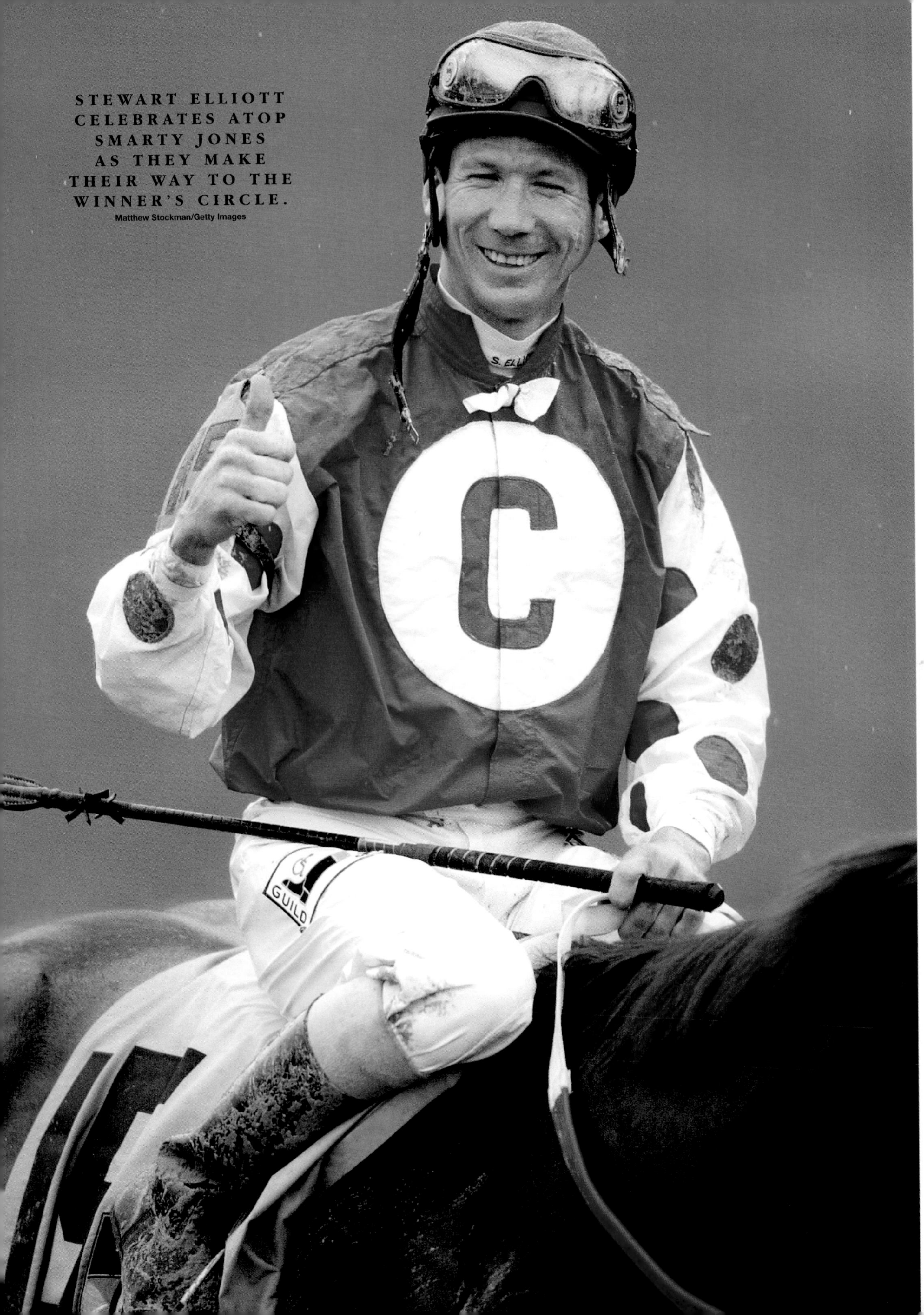

STEWART ELLIOTT CELEBRATES ATOP SMARTY JONES AS THEY MAKE THEIR WAY TO THE WINNER'S CIRCLE.

Matthew Stockman/Getty Images

SMARTY JONES
AND HIS HANDLERS
CELEBRATE AFTER
WINNING IN
LOUISVILLE.
Don Emmert/AFP/Getty Images

DERBY VICTORY IS ONE FOR THE AGES

BETH HARRIS

May 2, 2004

LOUISVILLE, KY. (AP)—Roy and Pat Chapman always wanted to win big races, so they named their stable Someday Farm.

That day arrived on a rainy Saturday at Churchill Downs when their undersized colt Smarty Jones ran through the mud for a 2³/₄-length victory in the Kentucky Derby.

"We never raced at this level; never thought we'd be here until we met Smarty," Chapman said.

That happened on February 28, 2001, the day the chestnut colt was born at Someday Farm in Chester County, Pennsylvania. He was named Smarty Jones after Pat Chapman's mother, Mildred Jones, who was nicknamed Smarty by her grandparents and was also born on a February 28.

But tragedy struck that December. Their trainer Bobby Camac and his wife were shot to death, and Camac's stepson was charged with double murder.

Camac had sued the stepson, Wade Russell, over allegations that Russell defrauded him of about $70,000 in a check-forgery scheme. No trial has been scheduled.

Distraught and concerned about Roy Chapman's deteriorating health, the couple disbanded their breeding operation after the slayings and sold all their horses except two: a 2-year-old and Smarty Jones.

At the time, the Chapmans had offers to sell Smarty Jones. But Pat, who buys horses based on the look in their eyes, told her husband, "Let's keep him."

"We just liked him," said 77-year-old Roy Chapman, who struggles for breath because of emphysema. "To see a horse that was born on the farm that we had and look at the stall he was born in, I'm still a little nervous."

In 2003, Smarty Jones was sent to small-time Philadelphia Park, where John Servis took over his training. Servis had been well-regarded by Camac.

"Without John Servis and Smarty's talents, we would not be here," Roy Chapman said.

He requires oxygen and uses a wheelchair to get around, although he stood up for a better view when the Derby began.

What a beautiful view it was. Smarty Jones stalked pacesetter Lion Heart for much of the 1¹/₄ miles, then pounced on him turning for home.

The Chapmans have been in the sport since the 1980s, but the big-time tracks and major money races always eluded them.

"I'm kind of numb," Pat Chapman said. "It's been an incredible journey."

Until Smarty Jones came along, the Chapmans' biggest boast in racing was I'll Get Along, who won 12 races and nearly $280,000 in her career. Perhaps her greatest gift was being the dam of Smarty Jones. I'll Get Along was later sold for $130,000.

The couple have since sold Someday Farm and moved to a smaller home, although they continue to breed and race in the farm's name. They own just four horses, with Smarty Jones being the star of their stable.

The Chapmans can afford to expand their operation now. The Derby victory was worth $854,800, and they got a $5 million bonus from Oaklawn Park because Smarty Jones swept the Rebel Stakes, Arkansas and Kentucky derbies.

Just before the race, Servis leaned over to Roy Chapman.

"Chap, whatever happens, we've had a great ride," he said.

"Absolutely, John, absolutely," the owner replied.

TRAINER JOHN SERVIS (LEFT), OWNERS PATRICIA AND ROY CHAPMAN (CENTER) AND JOCKEY STEWART ELLIOTT HOIST THE KENTUCKY DERBY TROPHY.
Matthew Stockman/Getty Images

"I'm kind of numb. It's been an incredible journey."

OWNER PAT CHAPMAN

"I couldn't ask to see him any brighter than he was this morning." TRAINER JOHN SERVIS

ON TO THE PREAKNESS

RICHARD ROSENBLATT

May 2, 2004

LOUISVILLE, KY. (AP) – Kentucky Derby winner Smarty Jones licked up his tub of feed, smacked around a net full of hay, looked "great" on Sunday, and is likely headed to the Preakness is two weeks.

The first undefeated Derby winner since Seattle Slew in 1977 was scheduled to be shipped to Philadelphia Park on Monday or Tuesday to begin resume training for the second leg of the Triple Crown.

The trip to Pimlico would be a few days before the May 15 race.

Derby runner-up Lion Heart will be there to have another try at the speedy Smarty Jones, with other Derby horses Limehouse, The Cliff's Edge and Borrego also being considered.

Limehouse, trained by Todd Pletcher, was fourth; The Cliff's Edge, trained by Nick Zito, was fifth; and Borrego was 10th.

Also expected for the 1³/₁₆ths-mile Preakness at Pimlico are Eddington and Rock Hard Ten, a pair of colts who did not have enough graded stakes earnings to run in the Derby, Cheiron and Water Cannon.

Cheiron is trained by 21-year-old Kristin Mulhall, who sent out Imperialism to a third-place finish in the Derby.

John Servis, who trains Smarty Jones said his little red colt "ate really good last night, played with the hay net and that's how he's come out of the earlier races.

"I couldn't ask to see him any brighter than he was this morning," he added.

Smarty Jones and Lion Heart turned what was supposed to be a wide-open Derby into a two-horse race.

Smarty Jones, with rookie Derby rider Stewart Elliott, aboard, caught the pacesetting Lion Heart near the top of the stretch and then pulled away to win the 1¹/₄-mile race by 2³/₄ lengths.

"My horse ran a great race, but he (Smarty Jones) was the better horse on the day," Lion Heart's trainer Patrick Biancone said, already back at Keeneland with his colt. "I have a world of respect for him. Smarty Jones could be anything."

While Smarty Jones is 7-for-7, with five starts this year, Lion Heart has just five career races—three this year.

Servis said the Pimlico course known for tight turns and a speed bias won't give Lion Heart an edge. However, he said Lion Heart "can easily go forward in a big way" since he's so lightly raced.

A few days before the Derby, Biancone told Servis he

SMARTY JONES GETS SOME LAST MINUTE GROOMING FROM MARIO
ARIAGAS BEFORE HEADING HOME TO PHILADELPHIA PARK.

WINNING THE KENTUCKY DERBY WAS ALL IN A DAY'S WORK FOR SMARTY JONES.
AP/WWP

expected a two-horse race between Speedy Jones and Lion Heart, and would make a good exacta bet.

"I said to all my owners and all my friends that at the half-mile pole it would be a two-horse race," Biancone said. "It would be my horse and Smarty Jones and I hope we can beat him. And that's just what happened."

Servis said if Smarty Jones is not training to his satisfaction, he wouldn't hesitate to pull him from contention.

"If he does go back to the track and I don't like the way he's training, then he's not going," Servis said. "If I'm not as confident as I was this week, we'll skip it. There are too many races down the line."

The Preakness is limited to 14 starters, but there has not been a full field since 1992.

48

MARIO ARRIAGAS AND SMARTY
JONES LEAVE BARN 42 AT
CHURCHILL DOWNS FOR THE
TRIP HOME.
AP/WWP

SMARTY JONES GIVES PHILADELPHIA A CHAMPION TO CHEER FOR

DAN GELSTON

May 3, 2004

BENSALEM, PA. (AP)—Stewart Elliott had trouble describing how it felt to dart across the finish line aboard Smarty Jones in the Kentucky Derby.

"It's something you have to experience to understand," he said.

That's where you lose most Philadelphia fans and athletes. They're unaccustomed to feting champions—or being champions.

A city yearning for a title from its disappointing big-bankroll pro teams—Eagles, Phillies, 76ers, Flyers—now has a hero in an undefeated 3-year-old colt and his Philly-area jockey, trainer and owners.

"I knew that everybody in the city and all the fans that come here all the time, everybody, was really hoping this horse could win," Elliott said Monday from Philadelphia Park—a trailer park compared to majestic Churchill Downs.

Suddenly, title-starved Philadelphia, where fans can be tougher than yesterday's cheesesteak and crankier than Phillies manager Larry Bowa, has found love in the underdog.

Sure, there was "Rocky" and the Villanova men's basketball team that won the national championship in 1985.

But this has been the year of the little teams—and colts—that could.

First, it was tiny Saint Joseph's that softened the blow of the Eagles' third straight loss in the NFC title game. It captivated college basketball with a 27-0 start and a run to the tournament's regional final.

"Everybody said this couldn't be done. The same thing with our team," said coach Phil Martelli, born and raised in the area. "I do find it entertaining. I'm pulling hard for them."

Monday was just another day at the track for Elliott, who was back at work riding low-grade horses. He never considered taking the day off, even though there have been worse reasons for begging off than winning the Kentucky Derby.

"I have a lot of good customers, a lot of good people to ride for here," he said. "It's just back to my job. I had the day off yesterday."

Smarty was expected to arrive at the park Tuesday night, along with trainer John Servis. Owners Roy and Pat Chapman returned to their home in Florida instead of their Someday Farm in Chester County, Pennsylvania.

As he walked to the paddock, Elliott was greeted with applause from about 100 fans, many of whom were decorated with Smarty Jones hats, buttons and shirts.

Jockeys who've competed against Elliott for years also clapped and offered congratulations. Nearby, a "Good Luck Smarty Jones" banner needed updating.

After Elliott finished fourth aboard The Fat Man in his first race—he won one of seven races—a fan shouted, "We love you anyway, Stew!"

Track announcer and park spokesman Keith Jones shrugged. "So much for the storybook," he said.

Still, life as an anonymous journeyman probably is over for Elliott. He was recognized Sunday at a Kentucky mall and signed autographs at the airport. When he arrived in Philadelphia, there were more fans and television cameras.

"This is bigger than the Eagles winning the Super Bowl because the Eagles are supposed to be there," said Jim Weber of Cinnaminson, N.J., who added that he won $500 betting on Smarty. "He wasn't supposed to be there. Horses from Philadelphia aren't supposed to be there."

SMARTY JONES AND EXERCISE RIDER PETE VAN
TRUMP ARE MET ON THE TRACK BY TRAINER
JOHN SERVIS DURING A PUBLIC WORKOUT AT
PHILADELPHIA PARK.

"We've got the horse right here, folks—a horse tailor-made for legend. Believe. Smarty Jones has been sent down from the racing gods with good news." — *IRA QUOTE*

WILL THIS BE 'THE SUMMER OF SMARTY JONES'?

JIM LITKE

May 3, 2004

LOUISVILLE, KY. (AP)—Every racehorse that captures the public's fancy has something more going for him than speed.

Secretariat galloped into America's heart in the summer of 1973, at a moment when the nation needed a diversion from the Vietnam War and Watergate. Five years later, Affirmed had Alydar, the most resolute of rivals. Four decades earlier, Seabiscuit boasted a rags-to-riches-story in the cruelest years of the Depression (and now he's got a movie, besides). Just last year, Funny Cide hijacked the sport of kings and turned it over to the subjects and court jesters for a few wacky weeks.

And now, along comes Smarty Jones.

"He seems to be the people's horse," jockey Stewart Elliott said in the gloaming of a rainy Kentucky afternoon, and he's not likely to get an argument on that point for the moment.

Minutes earlier, the undersized red chestnut with the decidedly commoner's pedigree had won the Kentucky Derby, reminding us that sometimes the best story also turns out to be the best horse on the first Saturday in May. Whether Smarty Jones will prove to be as resourceful in the Preakness and the Belmont—the two remaining gems of the Triple Crown—remains to be seen.

On the backstretch Sunday at Churchill Downs, his trainer wasn't even certain the colt would get the chance.

"If he does go back to the track and I don't like the way he's training, then he's not going," John Servis said. "If I'm not as confident as I was this week, we'll skip it. There are too many races down the line."

SMARTY JONES
IS RETURNED TO
HIS STALL AFTER
A WORKOUT.
AP/WWP

PHILADELPHIA PARK WELCOMES HOMETOWN HERO SMARTY JONES
AFTER HE WON THE KENTUCKY DERBY.
AP/WWP

"We've had a lot of offers and I've got the feeling we're going to get a couple more now. I think the price might have just gone up a little bit."

OWNER ROY CHAPMAN

But an argument can be made that there's already too much at stake for Smarty Jones not to attempt the most difficult trifecta in sports. Horse racing craves the buzz that a Triple Crown campaign pulls in its wake, and who better to provide it than the Pennsylvania-bred colt who nearly killed himself in a training accident last July, but recovered in time to lift a collection of racetrack lifers and regular guys to the pinnacle of their profession.

The last horse to sweep the Kentucky Derby, Preakness and Belmont was Affirmed, who held off Alydar in three suspense-filled battles over the span of five weeks in 1978. That gap is now one year longer than the previous longest drought between Triple Crown winners; the last sweep before Secretariat's transcendent romp in 1973 was Citation's summer of '48.

Funny Cide nearly turned the trick in 2003, and even if Smarty Jones runs all three and prevails, it won't restore racing's former glory. The days when the sport dueled only with baseball and boxing for the attention of the public are gone forever.

But for an afternoon or two more, it can restore the delicious anticipation of watching a performer try to take his game to a level where only history provides a proper context for judging. And who wouldn't be rooting to see someone finally take home the $5 million Triple Crown bonus that has never been claimed?

For better or worse, money won't influence Smarty Jones' connections. He has already earned a $5 million bonus by following up two Derby prep-season victories in Arkansas with his win at Churchill Downs. And besides, Roy Chapman, the 77-year-old Philadelphia car dealer who is taking the ride of his life, turned down offers of a blank check from several other owners who wanted to buy Smarty Jones even before the Derby.

"We've had a lot of offers and I've got the feeling we're going to get a couple more now," Chapman said after the Derby. "I think the price might have just gone up a little bit."

Barely three weeks earlier, Chapman was in a hospital with emphysema, the latest skirmish in a battle he's waged for more than a decade. His doctors weren't sure then whether he'd survive, let alone make the trip to Churchill Downs, but the thought of finally having a horse in the Derby had him feeling more alive than he had in months.

And Smarty Jones has already quickened the pace of Philadelphia, a town where Servis and Elliott are regarded by the local handicapping set as kings. They've worked together for nearly 20 years and combined for dozens of wins at gritty little Philadelphia Park, and a huge roar went up from the Phillies' crowd when the Derby was shown on the giant video screen before Saturday night's game.

"The city is embracing it," Servis said, "the whole state is embracing it."

And if Smarty Jones manages to win two more races in the coming weeks, the colt and his connections are going to be hard-pressed to make room for the rest of the crowd trying to jump on the bandwagon.

"Why Everybody Loves Smarty Jones. . .
The Horse from the Wrong Side of the Tracks
Looks Fit for a Triple Crown"

SPORTS ILLUSTRATED *COVER*

SMARTY JONES
AN *SI* COVER BOY

RICHARD ROSENBLATT

May 4, 2004

SMARTY JONES made quite an impression with his Kentucky Derby victory—on and off the racetrack.

While the Derby winner was on his way home to Philadelphia Park on Tuesday, his mud-splattered mug became cover boy material for *Sports Illustrated*, and yet another potential Preakness challenger pulled out of the race.

The photo of Smarty Jones and jockey Stewart Elliott racing ahead of the field in the Derby is accompanied by the headline: "Why Everybody Loves Smarty Jones ... The Horse from the Wrong Side of the Tracks Looks Fit for a Triple Crown."

It's been more than 20 years since a Derby winner made the *SI* cover. Sunny's Halo was the last, on the May 16, 1983, edition.

With his authoritative 2 3/4-length win over Lion Heart in the Derby to run his record to 7-0, Smarty Jones is also chasing away his rivals.

Cheiron, trained by Kristin Mulhall, was the latest Preakness defection, leaving six horses set to take on Smarty Jones in the May 15 second leg of the Triple Crown. On Monday, fourth-place Derby finisher Limehouse was ruled out by owner Cot Campbell.

Before Smarty Jones left Churchill Downs, trainer John Servis was beginning to understand how popular his colt has become.

"This is bigger than I ever imagined," Servis said. "It has been crazy, but I'm having the best time of my life."

Smarty Jones arrived at Baltimore-Washington International Airport early Tuesday evening and was loaded onto a trailer for his trip back home to Philadelphia Park.

Smarty Jones' popularity keeps growing as his story is told over and over again: He's a Pennsylvania-bred horse who nearly died when he slammed his head on an iron bar; his trainer and jockey are based at small-time Philly Park; and his owners refused a blank check to sell him.

Now he's the first undefeated Derby winner since Seattle Slew in 1977, with a chance to win the Preakness and enter the Belmont Stakes with a shot at becoming the first Triple Crown winner since Affirmed in '78.

He's also made millionaires of his owners, Roy and Pat Chapman. They collected a $5 million bonus from Oaklawn Park after Smarty Jones swept the Rebel Stakes, Arkansas Derby and Kentucky Derby.

"He's doing great," Servis said. "I see no reason why we wouldn't be heading to the Preakness. This story is great for our industry."

SMARTY JONES' MUD-SPLATTERED KENTUCKY DERBY WIN OVER LION HEART GRACED THE COVER OF *SPORTS ILLUSTRATED*.

AP/WWP

STEWART ELLIOTT IS CONGRATULATED BY FELLOW JOCKEYS AT PHILADELPHIA PARK AFTER RETURNING HOME VICTORIOUS FROM CHURCHILL DOWNS.

AP/WWP

OWNER JOHN CHAPMAN HOISTS THE KENTUCKY DERBY
TROPHY IN THE WINNER'S CIRCLE.

SMARTY JONES DRAWS A CROWD FOR RETURN HOME

May 5, 2004

BENSALEM, Pa. (AP)—Sal Sinatra never had a day like this.

The racing secretary at Philadelphia Park was scurrying around the barn area Wednesday morning, trying his best to maintain order on the first day of the Smarty Jones onslaught.

"We're working on the fly," Sinatra said. "We've never really had anything like this. It's just overwhelming."

At a track known for claiming races instead of champions, the morning unfolded without a hitch in greeting its Kentucky Derby winner.

There was a "Welcome Home Smarty Jones" cake and a big sign on trainer John Servis' barn congratulating him and owners Pat and Roy Chapman.

And there was a rare concession by horsemen that allowed Smarty Jones to have the track all to himself on a chilly and sunny morning.

"At 8:30, the track will remain closed for 15 minutes to let Smarty Jones train," bellowed a voice over the loudspeakers near Barn 11.

Ever hear of anything like that before?

Never, said Servis.

"They came to me with the idea, and it's awesome," Servis said, still smiling even after the long drive home from Louisville. "It shows you how much Philly Park loves this horse."

Perhaps track officials were just being cautious with Pennsylvania-bred horse Smarty Jones, the first undefeated Derby winner since Seattle Slew in 1977 and the likely favorite for the Preakness on May 15.

Because the quality of horses here is not up to the standards at major tracks such as Belmont Park, Churchill

SMARTY JONES AND PETE VAN TRUMP EXERCISE AT PHILADELPHIA PARK IN PREPARATION FOR THE PREAKNESS STAKES.
AP/WWP

"He was aggressive out there, that's good."

JOCKEY STEWART ELLIOT

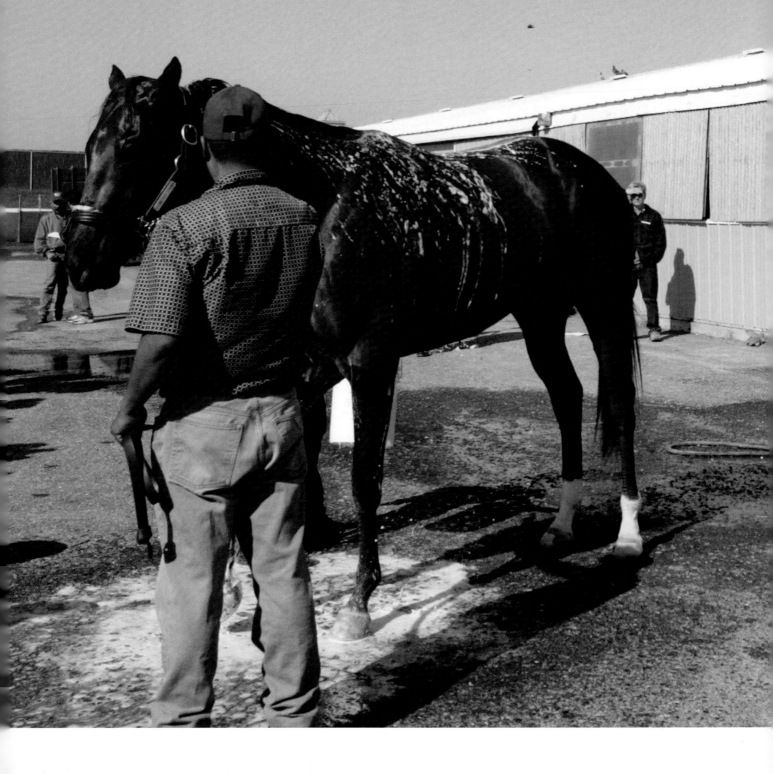

Downs or Santa Anita, there's no telling what could happen with a track full of cheap claimers running around with a Derby winner.

A media crowd totaling about 100—unheard of for a track that doesn't even have a press box—showed up for Smarty's first day home in about three months. The Pennsylvania bred trained up to the Derby in Arkansas, winning the Southwest Stakes, Rebel Stakes and Arkansas Derby before moving on to Kentucky.

So, on the morning after the Flyers advanced the Eastern Conference final in NHL playoffs, it was Smarty Jones' turn to take center stage in Philly.

With exercise rider Pete van Trump aboard, Smarty Jones emerged from the barn right on time. With a pony escort, Smarty Jones walked along the dirt path and made his way onto the track as a crowd of 200 including track personnel and media members took up spots along the outer rail for a close-up view.

It was a far cry from the 140,000 fans who turned out for the Derby, but a huge number on a dark day at a track lucky to draw over 1,000 on race days.

On his first trip to the track since his rousing $2^3/_4$-length win over Lion Heart last Saturday, Smarty Jones walked a half-mile, then jogged a half-mile. Then it was off the track, over to the barn for a sponge bath in front of dozens of TV cameras, and then back into stall 38.

Servis liked what he saw.

"He was nice and calm early on, just walking and looking around," Servis said. "And when he did jog off he was hitting the ground really good. He was a little on the muscle coming off the track and he's been eating real well."

Servis said Smarty Jones would gallop Thursday, but there won't be a final workout before the colt attempts to win the Preakness, setting up a Triple Crown try in the Belmont Stakes on June 5.

"The horse just ran a mile-and-a-quarter" in winning the Derby, Servis said. "He's dead fit. And he's coming right back in two weeks and, at that level, that's a lot to ask of a horse.

"Working him would be useless. He's already there. My big concern now is just keeping him happy. I want him to that stage where he's ready to go bear hunting with a switch. That's where I want him."

SMARTY JONES SHARES A LAUGH WITH PENNSYLVANIA GOVERNOR ED RENDELL, WHO VISITED SMARTY IN BENSALEM, PENNSYLVANIA.
AP/WWP

DERBY WINNER PICKS UP THE TRAINING PACE AT PHILLY PARK

RICHARD ROSENBLATT

May 6, 2004

BENSALEM, Pa. (AP)—Kentucky Derby winner Smarty Jones was back at the track Thursday morning, galloping an encouraging 1½ miles at Philadelphia Park in preparation for the Preakness Stakes.

Trainer John Servis rode his pony alongside Smarty Jones, and after the breeze over an empty track said his undefeated colt will pick up the pace Friday with a solo gallop.

"It'll be a big day to see how he handles himself," Servis said.

Smarty Jones, with exercise rider Pete van Trump aboard, returned to the track Wednesday for the first time since winning the Derby, walking a half-mile and jogging another half. Thursday's gallop was just a warm-up for the next few days of training.

"He did real good, I'm very happy," Servis said. "He got real strong at the end of the gallop, and I like to see that. At this stage, he's ready to do a little more than he's doing."

Servis intends to run Smarty Jones in the Preakness, but said Friday's gallop is critical because it will give the trainer a better idea how well his colt came out of last Saturday's Derby.

If Smarty Jones is not training as well as he did before the Derby, Servis already has said he won't hesitate to skip next Saturday's Preakness, the second leg of the Triple Crown.

Jockey Stewart Elliott, enjoying a day off after riding at Delaware Park on Wednesday, came to the track and watched Smarty Jones train.

"He was aggressive out there," Elliott said. "That's good."

Ever since Smarty Jones won the Derby, the Pennsylvania-bred has turned Philly into a one-horse town.

Yes, the Flyers are in the Eastern Conference finals of the NHL playoffs, but the horse with all the Philly connections—Servis, Elliott and owners Roy and Pat Chapman live in the area—is drawing unprecedented attention at a place that's merely a speck on the racing map.

While only about 50 people showed up to watch Smarty Jones on Thursday, a day after 200 were on hand for the colt's first day home in four months, bigger crowds are expected this weekend.

Track officials have invited the public to watch Smarty Jones gallop Saturday morning, followed by the mayor of Bensalem presenting the Chapmans with a key to the city.

On Sunday, Pennsylvania Gov. Edward Rendell is set to visit and honor Smarty Jones.

Servis said Smarty Jones will remain at Philly Park until next Thursday, when he will be shipped to Pimlico.

Smarty Jones has won all seven of his races and is the first undefeated Derby winner since Seattle Slew in 1977. A win in the 1³⁄₁₆th-mile Preakness would set up a third straight Triple Crown try in the Belmont Stakes on June 5. War Emblem in 2002 and Funny Cide last year both won the Derby and Preakness before falling short in the Belmont.

Smarty has already earned a $5 million bonus from Oaklawn Park for sweeping the Rebel Stakes, Arkansas Derby and Kentucky Derby. Should he become the first Triple Crown winner since Affirmed in 1978, Smarty would earn another $5 million bonus and top Cigar as racing's all-time leading money earner.

Smarty Jones' total earnings stand at $6,733,155.

SMARTY JONES AND
PETE VAN TRUMP WORK OUT
IN FRONT OF AN AUDIENCE
AT PHILADELPHIA PARK.
AP/WWP

A LARGE CROWD IN BENSALEM WATCHES
SMARTY JONES PREPARE FOR THE
PREAKNESS STAKES.
AP/WWP

"I just don't think there's anybody out there waiting for Smarty."

CO OWNER OF FUNNY CIDE JACK KNOWLTON

SMARTY JONES, FUNNY CIDE AND SEABISCUIT SPUR INTEREST IN SPORT OF KINGS

RON TODT

May 7, 2004

PHILADELPHIA (AP)—In the past year, the sport of kings has hit the trifecta.

A year ago, Funny Cide became the first gelding to win the Kentucky Derby since 1929 and went on to win the Preakness, becoming a contender for the first Triple Crown sweep in a quarter-century.

Meanwhile, a book and movie brought the tale of Depression-era underdog Seabiscuit to a new generation.

And now, Pennsylvania-bred Smarty Jones is the first undefeated Derby winner since Seattle Slew in 1977.

The three are "a happy confluence of events" that has brought horse racing to the forefront for people who otherwise wouldn't consider themselves racing fans, said Eric Wing, spokesman for the National Thoroughbred Racing Association.

The higher visibility couldn't come at a better time for an industry competing not only with other sports but with the spread of other forms of gambling—lotteries, casinos and American Indian gaming—and with new technology that could siphon away money.

Excitement has been created in five of the last seven years when one horse has won the Kentucky Derby and Preakness, going into the Belmont Stakes with a chance for the Triple Crown.

"If you knew a pitcher was going to take a perfect game into the ninth inning, chances are you'd tune in that game," Wing said. "That's how people perceive a Belmont Stakes when there's a Triple Crown on the line. It will instantly mean about four ratings points and create a nice spillover effect for the rest of the year."

Or even the following year. About 17 million people watched the Kentucky Derby last Saturday, a 16 percent increase over last year, which "probably speaks well to the Funny Cide/Seabiscuit effect," Wing said.

Tony DeMarco, service bureau director of Maryland-based Thoroughbred Racing Associations, gives partial credit to beefed-up industry and track marketing programs over the past five years, "but it certainly helps when you have the horses out there that are making headlines."

"We're doing pretty well on big days," said DeMarco, whose group represents 43 racing associations and 41 tracks. But "some tracks in this country do have to brace themselves for the days when they don't have these marquee events."

Officials in Pennsylvania, Maryland and New Jersey are lobbying for slot machines at racetracks after seeing horses, jockeys and bettors depart for richer purses in Delaware and West Virginia, both of which have slots.

In racing, success is measured not by attendance at the

SEABISCUIT AND JOCKEY GEORGE WOOLF LEAD WAR ADMIRAL AND
JOCKEY CHARLES KURTSINGER IN THE FIRST TURN AT PIMLICO IN 1938.
SEABISCUIT WON THE RACE AND SET A NEW TRACK RECORD.

ABOVE AND RIGHT: FUNNY CIDE
AND JOCKEY JOSE SANTOS CRUISE
TO VICTORY IN THE 129TH
KENTUCKY DERBY.
Jamie Squire/Getty Images

track—some don't even count heads and 85 percent of wagering is done offsite—but by betting handle, the total amount of money bet; the purse money won by the victors; and horse prices at auction. All three have been mostly trending up in the last few years, Wing said.

The handle has gone up every year since 1993, even with the spread of state lotteries and American Indian casinos, Wing said. Last year, the total amount wagered on thoroughbred racing in the United States was $15.2 billion, an increase of 0.08 percent, according to Jockey Club figures.

Gross purses grew for nine consecutive years and then dropped 1.7 percent last year. An NTRA task force is investigating why.

Finally, sales prices at auctions increased yearly from 1992 to 2000 and then dipped in the next two years, probably due to the bear market. But it rebounded last

year, which NTRA officials attribute not only to the recovering stock market but to the Funny Cide story.

"We've had a lot of interest in the past year, probably because of Funny Cide," said Gay Fisher, marketing and communications director of the Kentucky-based Thoroughbred Owners and Breeders Association, which has about 3,000 members. She is also executive director of the Greatest Game, an industry program aimed at attracting and aiding new investors to thoroughbred ownership.

Funny Cide's owners included a group of high school pals who rented yellow school buses to take them to the Triple Crown races. Smarty Jones' owner and jockey are based at small-time Philadelphia Park.

"People can relate to those guys and their lifestyles more than say ... (thoroughbred owners) who own jets and own oil companies," she said.

SMARTY JONES AND STEWART ELLIOTT ARE FESTOONED WITH
ROSES IN THE WINNER'S CIRCLE AT CHURCHILL DOWNS.
AP/WWP

SMARTY JONES HEADED FOR GREATNESS?

RICHARD ROSENBLATT

May 8, 2004

BENSALEM, Pa. (AP)—Going into the Kentucky Derby, there were so many questions about Smarty Jones that not even his perfect record seemed so impressive.

Here was this Pennsylvania-bred from downtrodden Philadelphia Park, with a sprinter's pedigree and a first-time Derby owner, trainer and jockey, who took the easiest path to Louisville by racing in Arkansas.

Even during his three-month stay at Oaklawn Park in Hot Springs, Arkansas, people would wander past John Servis' barn muttering: "This horse is from Philly Park? How good can he be?" the trainer recalled.

Pretty darned good it turns out. Maybe great.

When Smarty Jones ran away from Lion Heart in the final 220 yards and won the Kentucky Derby by 2 3/4 lengths on May 1, he became the first undefeated Derby winner since 1977 Triple Crown champion Seattle Slew.

The smallish red chestnut colt has won all seven starts by an average of 5.1 lengths. Only one challenger, Two Down Atomic in the Southwest Stakes, has finished within a length of the speedy Smarty.

Already, the colt's deeds are up there with racing greats like Seattle Slew and Spectacular Bid, who in 1979 was the last Derby winner trained and ridden by Derby first-timers.

"He's got a long way to go to fill those shoes," Servis said. "But the fact that they're using it in the same breath, that doesn't hurt my feelings any."

Back home at Philly Park this week, Smarty Jones is getting ready for next Saturday's Preakness, the 1 3/16th-mile race that may suit him better than the 1 1/4-mile Derby because it is known to favor speed horses.

While the Derby was considered wide open with an 18-horse field, it turned into a two-horse race in the slop at Churchill Downs. Lion Heart, who loves to run on the lead, will be back for another try in the Preakness, along with The Cliff's Edge (fifth) and Borrego (10th). Newcomers include Eddington, Rock Hard Ten and Water Cannon.

Servis is not too concerned with the competition.

"If he trains like he's trained going into the Derby, I'm going to be very confident," he said. "If he gets beat, he'll get outrun. There won't be any excuses."

A win in Baltimore and it's on to the Belmont Stakes three weeks later for a Triple try—the third straight and fifth in the past eight years. Greatness awaits.

That Smarty Jones has reached this point is truly amazing.

Only the second Pennsylvania-bred to win the Derby—Lil E. Tee in 1992 was the first—Smarty Jones arrived February 28, 2001, at Pat and Roy Chapman's Someday Farm in Chester County, Pennsylvania. The

AP/WWP

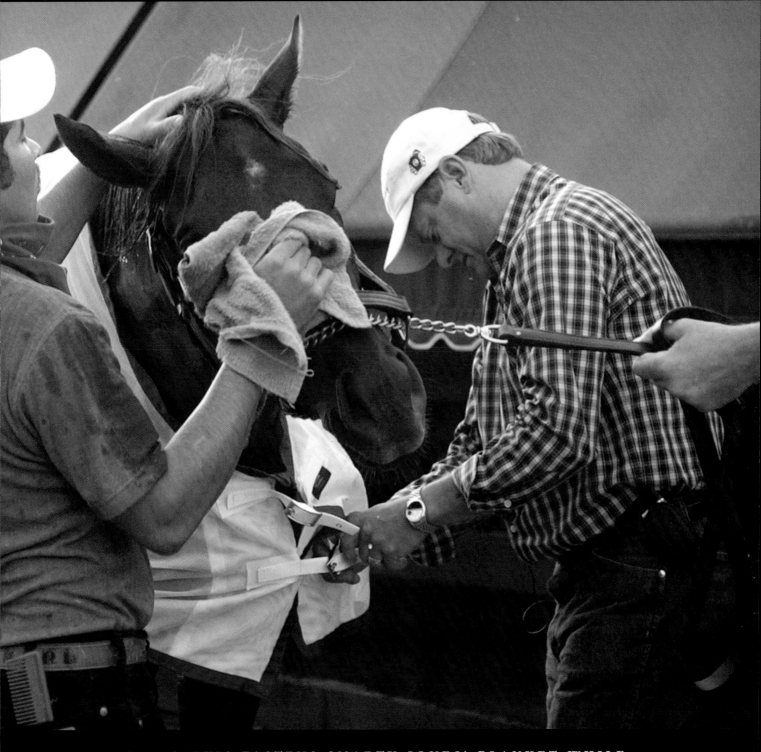

JOHN SERVIS FASTENS SMARTY JONES' BLANKET WHILE
THE GROOM DRIES HIS FACE AFTER HIS BATH.
AP/WWP

MARIO ARRIAGAS AND SMARTY JONES SHARE A QUIET MOMENT IN THE STALL AT PIMLICO BEFORE THE PREAKNESS.

AP/WWP

"Race after race, he still has fuel in the tank. Nobody's emptied it yet. Not even after a mile-and-a-quarter."

TRAINER JOHN SERVIS' FATHER, JOE SERVIS

colt was named for Pat Chapman's mother, Mildred, who was nicknamed "Smarty" and shared the same birthday.

A son of Elusive Quality, out of I'll Get Along, Smarty seemed destined to be a top sprinter. Elusive Quality set a world record for a mile on turf, as well as a track record for seven furlongs on dirt at Gulfstream Park in Florida. I'll Get Along, who won 12 of 39 races, is a daughter of sprint champion Smile.

Speed yes, but what about endurance? Joe Servis, John's dad and a former jockey, has an answer: He doesn't get tired.

"Race after race, he still has fuel in the tank," he said. "Nobody's emptied yet. Not even after a mile-and-a-quarter."

When he made it to the races, he was full of run. He won his maiden by five lengths at Philly Park on November 9.

After the race, jockey Stewart Elliott walked Smarty into the winner's circle. Elliott usually works out the horses he rides for Servis, a friend for more than 20 years. But this was his first time aboard Smarty.

When Servis walked over to congratulate Elliott, the rider leaned over and said: "Where you been hiding this one?"

The next start was a 15-length romp, then a victory in the dead of winter at Aqueduct before heading off to Arkansas.

The Chapmans were all for it. "They just told me to put a plan together that could get us to the Derby," Servis said.

Smarty loved Oaklawn. As the distance of each race increased, Smarty Jones grew stronger. He won the $1\frac{1}{16}$th-mile Southwest by three-quarters of a length and the Rebel by $3\frac{1}{4}$ lengths. With his Kentucky Derby status on the line—Smarty still hadn't run in a graded stakes race—he won the Arkansas Derby by $1\frac{1}{2}$ lengths in the rain.

Mickey Taylor, who owned Seattle Slew, watched the Derby on TV with interest. Slew loved to run, and hated for horses to be in front of him. He saw a little of that in Smarty Jones.

"He likes to run, and it looks like he really enjoys it," Taylor said. "He looks like the real McCoy."

WILL SMARTY STILL BE PARTYING AFTER PREAKNESS?

JIM LITKE

May 14, 2004

AP/WWP

NO MAJOR championship in sports has a shorter shelf life than the Kentucky Derby.

Win the Masters, as Phil Mickelson did in April, and you can dine out free in the green jacket every night for two months before golf's next Grand Slam event.

Win the World Series, an NBA, NFL or NHL championship, and the party can last an entire offseason. Win Olympic gold and it's a good three years before anyone even thinks to ask, "What have you done for me lately?"

But win the Derby and the grace period lasts exactly two weeks. There's barely time for even one good hangover, as Smarty Jones and his connections are finding out.

"This is going to be the toughest race he has had," trainer John Servis said on the eve of Saturday's Preakness.

Some people would argue he doesn't know the half of it. On the other hand, being newcomers to the top echelon of racing and the unique demands of a Triple Crown might be the best thing Smarty Jones' campaigners have going for them.

Sweeping the sport's three biggest races in five weeks is perhaps the toughest feat in sports. One measure of that is the 26 years that have elapsed since Affirmed last turned the trick, holding off Alydar in consecutive thrillers at the Derby, Preakness and Belmont.

Secretariat managed to do the same just five years earlier, but that transcendent romp came after a 25-year drought, dating to Citation's summer of '48.

But time isn't the only measure of difficulty. Once known as the "sport of kings," racing has been off the throne for so long that the search for a superstar has turned into a parody of *American Idol*.

Five times in the previous seven years, a horse left the Preakness with two wins under its belt and a shot at the Triple—only to be exposed by the marathon distance of the Belmont.

Last year, the Triple Crown wannabe was a quirky gelding named Funny Cide, whose decidedly common pedigree and hoi polloi ownership group made for a great story.

Their pursuit of the trifecta got an unexpected lift as author Laura Hillenbrand's book *Seabiscuit* topped the best-seller list and headed for the silver screen. In retrospect, more attention was probably the last thing Funny Cide needed.

A year ago, just moments after the gelding captured the Preakness, trainer Bob Baffert stood along the runway to the paddock and surveyed the gray sky above the Pimlico Race Course. Three times since 1997, he was in the same position as Funny Cide's connections and he knew only too well what awaited them around the bend.

"Your life is under glass, you open yourself up to every kind of second-guessing, your voice is shot, everything still has to go perfect for you to have a chance—and then you get beat by a nose," he recalled.

Which is exactly what happened to Real Quiet, the second of his three Triple Crown contenders.

"That's why I can't wait to get home," Baffert said, "and watch somebody else go through it on TV."

The somebody else this time around is Servis, jockey Stewart Elliott and owners Ray and Pat Chapman. And to their credit, just like the Triple Crown rookies around Funny Cide, they haven't big-timed anybody since their brush with fame.

Elliott took just one day off after winning the Derby, reporting for duty the following Monday at Philadelphia Park, and climbing board the same cheap mounts he rode for most of his career.

Servis, who like Elliott was largely unknown outside the confines of the ramshackle Philly venue, brought Smarty Jones back two days later amid all kinds of backslapping.

"This is bigger than I ever imagined," Servis said. "It has been crazy, but I'm having the best time of my life."

He and everybody connected to Smarty Jones certainly earned it. The shame is that the only way it continues is by winning Saturday, and then again three weeks later in New York.

Whether Smarty Jones senses the pressure is anyone's guess. But the Preakness will be his fifth race in 11 weeks, and that wear and tear is only one of the obstacles the colt will have to overcome.

He'll have to beat four of the same horses he battled at Churchill Downs—now that fifth-place finisher The Cliff's Edge was scratched Friday because of injury—and five entries who took the grueling Derby weekend off.

On top of that, Servis doesn't know if the weather forecast for Pimlico—isolated thunderstorms, temperatures in the mid-80s—will create the same sloppy conditions that Smarty Jones enjoyed in the Derby.

What he does know is that he's got the horse to beat. And even though Smarty Jones went off as the favorite at the Derby, the undersized chestnut will be carrying a lot more than the weight of a jockey this time out. And Servis wasn't above piling on, either.

"If we get through this," he said Thursday about his shot at the Triple Crown, "I think we'll have a really good chance at it."

STEWART ELLIOT PRAISES
SMARTY JONES AS THEY CROSS
THE FINISH LINE TO WIN THE
129TH PREAKNESS STAKES.

Tim Sloan/AFP/Getty Images

"I had another gear left. Unfortunately, when I hit the other gear, Smarty Jones had about four more gears." JOCKEY GARY STEVENS, RIDER OF RUNNER-UP ROCK HARD TEN

SMARTY JONES WINS PREAKNESS, TRIPLE CROWN TRY UP NEXT

RICHARD ROSENBLATT

May 16, 2004

BALTIMORE (AP)—The move came in a flash.

Lion Heart had the lead, Smarty Jones was lurking and jockey Stewart Elliott was waiting for the right moment to go. The Preakness was setting up according to plan.

Around the far turn, Elliott angled his Kentucky Derby winner to the inside of the pacesetter, and the horses entered the stretch together.

And then the race was over.

With one breathtaking surge, Smarty Jones left the field far behind, his lead building with every powerful stride over the final eighth of a mile. By the time he crossed the finish line, the little chestnut colt had delivered a record $11\frac{1}{2}$-length victory to set the stage for a dramatic Triple Crown try at the Belmont Stakes in three weeks.

"I had another gear left. Unfortunately, when I hit the other gear, Smarty Jones hit about four more gears," said Gary Stevens, who was aboard runner-up Rock Hard Ten. "Smarty Jones looks like he's just getting warmed up right here at the finish."

Even after $1\frac{3}{16}$ miles on a hot and hazy afternoon at Pimlico, the undefeated Smarty was still running hard well beyond the finish line. The Belmont is $1\frac{1}{2}$ miles, the longest of the Triple Crown races, but there seems to be no stoppin' him now.

"I have a good horse, but that was a great horse that beat us," Rock Hard Ten's trainer, Jason Orman, said.

Elliott won't quibble with that.

"He's just unbelievable. He just keeps getting better, this son of a gun. I mean, he just did it so easy," the jockey said.

Smarty Jones is eight-for-eight with one to go in his bid to become just the 12th Triple Crown champion and the first to sweep the Derby, Preakness and Belmont since Affirmed in 1978.

He would also claim another $5 million bonus and become racing's richest horse.

By trouncing nine rivals, Smarty Jones simply added another amazing chapter to racing's feel-good story of the year.

The record crowd of 112,668 roared when Elliott asked this sensational Pennsylvania-bred to make his winning move. Down the stretch, the 39-year-old rider merely tapped him with the whip twice in the final eighth-of-a-mile, and Smarty took off like a shot. The margin of victory topped the record of 10 lengths by Survivor in 1873, in the first Preakness.

Lion Heart, runner-up in the Derby, faded to fourth. Rock Hard Ten, in just his fourth start, finished strong for second ahead of Eddington. Imperialism was fifth, followed by Sir Shackleton, Borrego, Little Matth Man, Song of the Sword and Water Cannon.

"Smarty Jones, man, he's just an amazing horse," said Mike Smith, who was aboard Lion Heart. "I think me and Gary are on some great colts, just born in the wrong years."

Winning time for the race was 1:55.59, well off the record of 1:53.40 held by Louis Quatorze (1996) and Tank's Prospect (1985).

The overpowering win put in place some mind-bog-

gling possibilities for the 3-year-old who has captured America's fancy—as Funny Cide did last year before his Triple Crown bid fell short in the Belmont.

Smarty Jones will be the sixth horse in the last eight years with a Triple chance, but there's a big difference this time around: Smarty is the only one who hasn't lost.

"He came through for America. I'm so impressed with his effort," trainer John Servis said. "I knew he had to bring his best game. I knew this was the toughest race he was going to be in in a long time. And he brought it. He brought it big time."

So much so that Stevens compared him to one of the greatest of champions of all time.

"Smarty reminded me of Secretariat, the way he pulled away," he said.

A victory in the Belmont and Smarty Jones would join Seattle Slew as the only Triple Crown winners with unbeaten records. Smarty, like Slew in 1977, would be 9-for-9.

The son of Elusive Quality would also surpass Cigar as the richest racehorse in North America. Smarty would earn a $5 million bonus from Visa with a Triple Crown sweep. Add his purse money, plus the $5 million bonus he already earned from Oaklawn Park for winning the Rebel Stakes, Arkansas Derby and Kentucky Derby, and Smarty's total would top $13 million. Cigar earned $9,999,815.

Smarty Jones, the 3-5 favorite, earned $650,000 for winning the Preakness, boosting his career total to $7,383,155—fourth on the all-time list.

Owned by Pat and Roy Chapman, Smarty returned $3.40, $3 and $2.60. Rock Hard Ten paid $5 and $4. Eddington, with Jerry Bailey aboard, paid $5.20.

Smarty became racing's best story even before the Derby because of his soap-opera history: He nearly died when he slammed his head on an iron bar; his trainer and jockey are based at small-time Philadelphia Park; and the Chapmans once refused a blank check to sell him. Roy is

Since the Derby, it's been one Smarty party after another. The horse got a hero's welcome when he returned to Philly Park, where about 5,000 fans showed up to watch

him jog around the track.

Perhaps no one is enjoying the party more than the Chapmans. Roy, who turned 78 three days after the Derby, uses a wheelchair and needs an oxygen supply tank to help with his emphysema.

Smarty's success, he says, has energized him.

"Some day, somewhere, he's going to get beat," Roy Chapman said. "We're trying to put that off as long as we can."

And now it's on to the Belmont on June 5, where New York Racing Association officials are expecting "the biggest day in New York racing history," NYRA senior vice president Bill Nader said.

Servis says Smarty will be there "as long as he tells us he's ready."

The largest crowd for a Belmont was 103,222 in 2002, when Derby and Preakness winner War Emblem stumbled at the start and finished eighth.

Among the challengers Smarty could face are Derby starters Birdstone, Friends Lake, Master David, Read the Footnotes and Tapit. Other possible starters include Mustanfar, Relaxed Gesture, Sinister G and Royal Assault, who won the Sir Barton on the Preakness undercard.

"He'll do whatever I want him to do," Elliott said, referring to the Belmont's demanding distance. "It won't be a problem."

The jockey has handled his newfound fame well, but he's

SMARTY JONES SPEEDS TO THE FINISH AND MAINTAINS HIS UNDEFEATED STATUS.
Tim Sloan/AFP/Getty Images

also encountered the downside of being in the spotlight.

Elliott admitted Friday that he battled alcoholism several years ago. The revelation came after Kentucky racing officials fined Stewart $1,000 for failing to disclose on his Derby application that he pleaded guilty in 2001 to an assault charge. That same year, the jockey also pleaded guilty to charges of assault and criminal mischief involving a former girlfriend.

"I just think about the past and I look where I was and now, the future," Elliott said. "Look where I am."

THE FIELD IS LEFT EATING DUST
AS SMARTY JONES WINS THE
PREAKNESS BY 11 ¹/₂ LENGTHS.

"I peeked back and nobody was coming."

JOCKEY STEWART ELLIOT AFTER THE KENTUCKY DERBY

A REAL SMARTY THIS SMARTY JONES

JIM LITKE

May 16, 2004

BALTIMORE (AP) – Forget for a second how masterful the Preakness win was. This is how smart a horse Smarty Jones really is: He made sure the easiest moments of jockey Stewart Elliott's week turned out to be the race itself.

"It didn't seem to matter where I was on the track, my horse was running so easy," Elliott said. "So I just took him inside and he did the rest."

Athletes in trouble talk all the time about how the field of play is their sanctuary. For the span of just under two minutes on a hot, hazy Saturday afternoon, Smarty Jones cut through the chaos reigning on every side of him and turned Pimlico Race Course into a safe haven for his rider.

The two weeks between the Kentucky Derby and the Preakness should have been time for Stewart to savor the biggest achievement of his career, to tell the story of how a 39-year-old jockey stuck in the bush-leagues doesn't lose faith with his sport, then gets his one shot at the big time and delivers beyond anyone's imagination.

That's how the post-Derby week began. Elliott went back to Atlantic City and Philadelphia and rode cheap mounts to pay back all the people who told him to never give up.

Then came news that Elliott had failed to disclose an assault charge on a form for Churchill Downs, an omission that cost him a $1,000 fine. Then came reports of another assault charge, and one of racing's most enchanting tales seem to be unraveling faster than the braid on a show horse's mane.

On the eve of the Preakness, Elliott confronted the whispers. He walked into the press box at Pimlico and stood before a dozen or so reporters. He took every question and answered each one by looking his questioner in the eye.

"I have nothing to hide. I've had a lot of personal problems and done some things that I'm not proud of," Elliott said. "But that's behind me. I want to just look ahead to the future. Hopefully, all that mess is behind me. All of what happened was because of the alcohol."

Elliott hasn't had a drink in nearly four years, he said, though he also admitted he hasn't been to an Alcoholics Anonymous meeting in six months. You could almost say success has been getting in the way.

He climbed aboard Smarty Jones at the beginning of the prep races leading to the Kentucky Derby and won all six of those. And just when it seemed Elliott couldn't ride any better than he did at the Derby, he did.

Stalking Lion Heart just as he had at Churchill Downs, Elliott was content to let Smarty Jones dictate his own pace. And despite the wildly cheering crowd lining the rail and the thundering hooves behind him, Elliott never felt more in control. He knew heading into the far turn that all he had to do was get by Lion Heart and into the clear and the race was his.

Before the Derby, more than a few people would have argued that Elliott didn't belong on the same track as Lion Heart's jockey, Mike Smith. As it turned out, they only shared this one for a few moments and it was Elliott who taught his big-name counterpart the lesson.

Just when it seemed Smarty Jones' momentum might

carry him too far wide to make up enough ground to grab the lead, Elliott took the undersized chestnut to the rail and left Smith and Lion Heart to deal with his dust.

Once he got the lead, the outcome was never in question.

"I peeked back and nobody was coming," Elliott said.

He had the whip ready in his hand, but there was no reason to use it.

"I never turned my stick over. I tapped him two or three times, just to let him know it was time to go," Elliott said, "and that was all he needed."

And a chance was all Elliott ever needed.

"When he was getting aboard my horse in the Kentucky Derby, I think somebody called him Stew Who? a novice rider," said Roy Chapman, Smarty Jones' 78-year-old owner. "Well you just heard a description of this race. If that sounds like a novice rider, I'll kiss your you-know-what."

A more apt comparison might be made with Red Pollard, the jockey whose story was told in the movie *Seabiscuit*. Like Pollard, Elliott was willing to scrap and scrape for his chance, to climb aboard bad horses at even worse tracks because riding was the only thing he ever wanted to do.

Through injuries and his struggle with drinking, when he was racing for $400 purses at state fairs and stuck in a sweatbox just trying to make weight, Elliott never gave up. And just like Pollard, he has found the horse that made the fight worthwhile.

"I just think about the past and I look where I was and now, the future," Elliott said, letting out a low whistle. "Look where I am."

He's headed to New York with a chance at the Triple Crown, becoming the sixth jockey in eight years to take a shot at one of the most fabled achievements in sports. All of them were better known. But Elliott only has to be better than they were on one more Saturday afternoon to find out what it feels like when the game loves you every bit as much you love it.

THE CHAPMANS CELEBRATE WITH SMARTY JONES IN
THE WINNER'S CIRCLE AT PIMLICO RACE TRACK.

> ## "As long as he tells us he's ready, we're on to the Belmont." *TRAINER JOHN SERVIS*

EVEN SERVIS IS SURPRISED ABOUT SMARTY

DAVID GINSBURG

May 16, 2004

BALTIMORE (AP) – John Servis was still glowing over Smarty Jones' spectacular performance Saturday when someone told him the margin of victory was a Preakness Stakes record.

Servis raised his eyebrows, wiped his brow and smiled.

Seems as if there's no end to the surprises Smarty Jones has for his proud trainer, owners Roy and Patricia Chapman and the rest of the horse-racing world.

Smarty Jones wouldn't be going to the Belmont if he had lost in the Preakness, but his 11½-length victory means he'll have a chance to become the first horse to win the Triple Crown since Affirmed in 1978.

"As long as he tells us he's ready, we're on to the Belmont," Servis declared.

After Smarty Jones rolled to victory in the Kentucky Derby, Servis decided he would go easy on his undefeated horse in preparing for the Preakness. Smarty Jones had already run five races in 2004, and Servis realized the chestnut colt desperately needed a break.

"The only change for me was in his training," he said. "We did a whole lot less with him."

Like any good trainer, Servis discussed strategy with jockey Stewart Elliott before the race. It was a brief conversation in the paddock.

"I said it looked like it was going to be the same race as the Derby," Servis said. "When you've got a rider like this, just let him go out there and do his job."

At the Derby, the excitement almost seemed too much for the 78-year-old Chapman, who had to take a series of deep breaths to calm himself after his horse's victory. He stays hooked up to an oxygen tank because of emphysema, and he uses a wheelchair.

For the Preakness, Chapman was able to keep his emotions in check.

"I made my mind up I was going to try to stay a little calmer," he said. "I was really pretty calm. I had to hold back tears a little bit. Really, emotionally it hit me just how good this horse is."

It's something to sleep on, for sure.

"I was like John. I didn't sleep too good last night," Chapman said. "There were a lot of good horses in this race. I thought he might win, but I never thought he would blow them away. I'm just happy."

Someone asked Chapman if he ever saw Seabiscuit, who ran in the late 1930s. The venerable owner took the question in stride.

"I trained him!" Chapman quipped, winking at his wife, Patricia.

Upon taking the job of training Smarty Jones, Servis nearly ruined him. When he took the horse to the starting gate for the first time, Smarty Jones reared up, banged his head on an iron bar and knocked himself unconscious.

Servis has since become much more adept at handling the horse.

"I was obviously concerned going into the race," he said. "Someone asked me this morning if I was as confident as I was going into the Derby, and I said no, I was not. I think he's a little vulnerable."

Hardly.

Smarty Jones made it eight wins in eight career races with remarkable ease, taking control before the stretch and galloping to an overpowering victory.

"Smarty Jones is obviously a super horse," said Imperialism owner Steve Taub, who watched his horse lose for the second time in two weeks. "He had his ears pinned back, and it looked like he was just having a ball out there. He's just a spectacular racehorse."

Good enough to make Servis' job pretty easy.

"Once again, everything I'm asking for, he's stepped up to the plate," he said. "I'm so impressed with his effort today, I really am. I knew he had to bring his best game. I knew this was the toughest race he was going to be in for a long time. And he brought it. He brought it big time."

And now it's on to the Belmont. But first, Servis will take Smarty Jones back to Philadelphia, where all the attention should get rather hectic.

Luckily for Servis, his wife, Sherry, will make sure he doesn't get more overworked than the horse.

"After the Derby, once we got back to Philly things were so nerve-wracking," Servis said. "It took about 24 hours, and my wife stepped in and said, 'I'm going to get an appointment book and I'm going to work it out.'

"She's done a great job. I'm sure she'll continue to do a great job the next three weeks. That's why we're a great team."

"Yes, Virginia, there is a Smarty Jones."

FAN QUOTE

SERVIS TOUCHED BY HOW SMARTY JONES HAS TOUCHED OTHERS

DAN GELSTON

May 21, 2004

BENSALEM, PA. (AP) – The letters, calls and e-mails arrive so fast that John Servis can't keep up.

They come from schools and prisons, and even those who never watched a horse race until they heard about Smarty Jones. The little red chestnut colt that Servis led to wins in the Kentucky Derby and Preakness has made even the casual fans want to be a part of Smarty Mania.

"It's amazing how much this horse has touched so many people's lives," Servis said. "I expected this would be like a sporting event where people scream and holler. It's more like, 'thank you so much.' People are excited to have this story to grasp on to."

Smarty Jones' popularity only keeps growing. Servis and wife, Sherry, said they'll answer all the well wishers, but it's taking time. Fans send religious passages or stories about how the horse has changed their life. Grade school children send drawings and ask questions about how Smarty Jones felt when he was hurt.

"So many young kids have grasped onto it, which gives you hope that the next generation can be thrust into the racing world and be fans," Servis said.

Some requests, though, have lacked horse sense. There are the requests for Smarty's autograph, a marriage proposal (yes, for the horse), an equine message therapist has offered a rubdown, and even a psychic wanted to lay her hands on the horse to get a prediction.

Hmmm, Smarty to win, perhaps?

Servis has turned into a minor celebrity, appearing on countless radio and TV shows. He won a fan a prize on a radio contest in California on Friday for answering trivia questions correctly. The hosts didn't even ask him about his colt.

"I didn't even know they had radios in some of these towns," Servis said, laughing.

His name may as well have been Smarty since that's what Flyers fans chanted when they saw Servis at the Game 6 playoff game on Thursday night. Servis, a die-hard Flyers fan who donned a team jersey during a public workout, met some of the players before the game and they wanted his autograph.

Servis also met the widow of former Flyers announcer Gene Hart. She told Servis that she rarely left the house since her husband died, but on the day of the Preakness she drove to Atlantic City to bet on Smarty Jones.

"She just said, 'Thank you so much,'" Servis said. "That's the kind of story it is."

Emlen School
Chew Ave + Upsalst
Philadelphia Pa
May 20th 2004

Dear Smarty Jones,

Eat good oats so you can win the next race.

Next week I will wach the race on tv.

I am your number 1 fan.

You ran as fast as a dog.

My little sister like you to,

your friend

Nasir

YOUNG FANS GATHER AT SMARTY JONES' HOME TRACK TO WISH HIM SUCCESS AT THE BELMONT STAKES.
AP/WWP

> *"So many young kids have grasped onto it, which gives you hope that the next generation can be thrust into the racing world and be fans."*
>
> TRAINER JOHN SERVIS

It's a story that Servis hopes ends with a Belmont Stakes win and the first Triple Crown winner since Affirmed in 1978.

Smarty Jones had a strong, solo $1\frac{1}{2}$-mile gallop early Friday morning at Philadelphia Park. The horse could take longer gallops next week and Servis planned to work the horse at least once before the Belmont.

Meanwhile, four horses that could be in the Belmont Stakes are among those running in Saturday's Peter Pan Stakes at Belmont. Master David and Friends Lake, who both finished far behind Smarty at the Kentucky Derby, were entered, along with Purge and Sinister G. Purge finished behind Smarty Jones in the Rebel Stakes and Arkansas Derby, while Sinister G lost to the Derby and Preakness winner in the Count Fleet Stakes at Aqueduct in January.

Servis remained undecided on when to ship his colt to New York and said he could even wait until the day before the June 5 race.

Smarty Jones has another public gallop at 8:30 a.m Saturday. Nearly 5,000 fans poured into Philadelphia Park to watch his last workout two weeks ago. Track officials are expecting a larger crowd this time.

Everyone wants a peek at the horse that has captured the public's fancy—and could be coming to a theater near you.

The family has started receiving pitches about book and movie deals wanting to turn Smarty's tale into an update of Seabiscuit. Servis wants Kiefer Sutherland to play him; his 13-year-old son, Tyler, said he'd play jockey Stewart Elliott.

Still, Sherry Servis said her husband is starting to feel worn down from all the newfound obligations. It's a small price to pay for being the main event in the racing story of the year.

"I'm sure after the Belmont it will die down and it will be back to a normal life," she said.

"It's great to come out here today, put your problems aside and enjoy the blessings life has to offer. We need a hero and Smarty is our hero. He has united people." FAN QUOTE

SMARTY JONES MAKES PRACTICE RUN BEFORE CROWD OF 8,500

May 22, 2004

BENSALEM, PA. (AP) – Smarty Jones came to the home stretch with his head lowered, focused on each stride.

Seemingly oblivious to the thousands of fans who packed Philadelphia Park's grandstand, the Kentucky Derby and Preakness winner galloped on to a rousing ovation Saturday.

In his first public run since winning the Preakness last week, Smarty Jones galloped 1½ miles under exercise rider Pete van Trump before an estimated crowd of 8,500.

"It's a joy to me to see the people come out and flock around this horse like they do," trainer John Servis said. "It's great for the whole industry. I just hope it carries on and continues to roll."

After winning the Derby, Smarty Jones returned to his hometown track and a crowd roughly half the size of Saturday's showed up for a public run May 8.

Smarty Jones will attempt to become the first Triple Crown winner since Affirmed in 1978 when he runs in the Belmont Stakes on June 5.

Fans began lining up before sunrise for their chance to see the little red chestnut colt, and grab as many free doughnuts and as much not-so-free Smarty merchandise as they could get.

Among the first in line was racing fan Bill Perentau, who claims to have been at the front gate at 5:13 a.m.

"I don't know if you can call it bandwagon jumping," Perentau said. "And it doesn't matter where this horse is from. Whether it's Philly or Bensalem or wherever. It's the horse and jockey that matter."

Servis was pleased with what he saw, but is watching Smarty Jones closely to make sure the colt doesn't work too hard.

"You have to watch it with him because he wants to train so hard, and you have to watch that he doesn't over-train himself," Servis said. "It's always a day-to-day thing. Today was awesome. I mean he relaxed so good."

Fans had their reasons for rising before dawn to watch a three-minute gallop. Some view Smarty Jones as a possible end to Philadelphia's 21-year major-championship drought, others believe the colt means much more.

"It's great to come out here today, put your problems aside and enjoy the blessings life has to offer," Carol O'Brien said. "We need a hero and Smarty is our hero. He has united people."

A LARGE CROWD GATHERS AT PHILADELPHIA
PARK TO WATCH SMARTY JONES WORK OUT.
AP/WWP

SMARTY JONES AND PETE VAN TRUMP MAKE A PRACTICE RUN IN FRONT OF A CROWD OF 8,500.
AP/WWP

"Philadelphia is starving for a winner."

BENSALEM MAYOR JOSEPH DiGIROLAMO

SMARTY JONES SPARKS TURF WAR

Philly And Bensalem Lay Claim To Horse

May 27, 2004

BENSALEM, PA. (AP) – Smarty Jones may need a new nickname. The Kentucky Derby and Preakness winner has been dubbed the "Philly Flash" or the "Philly Flyer" while being presented to the country as Philadelphia's first sports champion in more than two decades.

One problem. Turns out, the ol' Philly Flyer is from … Bensalem?

Where?

Until about two months ago, Bensalem Township, an area of 21 square miles, was the buffer township between Philadelphia on the West and the rest of Bucks County on the East and Northeast. Now it's the town that wants its horse back.

"We want our recognition," Bensalem Mayor Joseph DiGirolamo said.

Odds are, no one will start calling Smarty Jones the "Bensalem Blazer" anytime soon. It hasn't helped that Smarty Jones' home in Bensalem is called Philadelphia Park.

But the township is staking a claim to Smarty in this turf war.

DiGirolamo wants to rename one of Bensalem's main thoroughfares after its main thoroughbred, hoping to turn Street Road into "Smarty Jones Boulevard." Philadelphia Park is located on Street Road.

"Philadelphia is starving for a winner," DiGirolamo said. "They can grasp at it, but they need to remember it's in Bensalem and not just Philly."

Who can blame Philadelphia sports fans for wanting to latch on to this undefeated colt?

They shed tears over lost Stanley Cups. They bemoan the big-game failures of big-time teams. They call the all-sports station and yakety-yak a blue streak. They watch the city build new ballparks but rarely see championships.

Then along comes Smarty Jones, the plucky horse that needs only a win in the June 5 Belmont Stakes for the first Triple Crown since 1978.

Bensalem started snorting when Pennsylvania Gov. Ed Rendell called the colt's Preakness win a great day for Philadelphia, and the city council started talking about a parade down Broad Street—which hasn't staged a celebration for a pro sports team since the 76ers in 1983.

"The governor is from Philadelphia. What do you expect him to do?" DiGirolamo said.

"He's a horse that America loves."

TRAINER JOHN SERVIS

City newspapers and news broadcasts have made only cursory mentions of Bensalem, if at all, but the connection to Bensalem runs deeper than Smarty Jones.

Trainer John Servis has lived in Bensalem for parts of almost 24 years and jockey Stewart Elliott also lives in Bucks County. So does exercise rider Pete Van Trump. And while owners Pat and Roy Chapman have car dealerships in Philadelphia, they reside just outside the city.

Servis has tried to stay out of the debate.

"He's a horse that America loves," Servis said. "I think he belongs to everybody. Everybody can root for this horse. It doesn't matter where you're from."

But it's been a burr under the saddle for those in Bensalem who want Philadelphians to take their cheesesteaks and stuff it.

"They keep saying it's Philly's horse. It hasn't done much for Bensalem," said Ellis Saltzman, of Bensalem. "Philadelphia should back off."

At the Great American Diner and Pub across the street from Philadelphia Park, fans on a weekday afternoon can watch racing simulcasts on big screens near the bar. Bartender Ryan Calcagni said the diner has been packed during Smarty Jones' races, but wonders how soon the hoopla will die down.

"Right now, everyone loves the horse and it's been great for everyone around here," he said. "But I wonder if we rename the street, in a couple of years it will be, 'Who's Smarty Jones?'"

Sen. Robert Tomlinson, a Bucks County Republican, said renaming the street wasn't a sure bet.

"I think we'd have to think about it. There's an awful lot of business along Street Road," Tomlinson said.

In a downtown Philadelphia bar, some patrons accused Bensalem of sour grapes.

"I think they should get a life. Who ever heard of Bensalem?" said Harry Williford. "They don't even play good high school football there. It's a Philadelphia horse. It's Philadelphia Park."

Tomlinson said Smarty Jones has lifted the spirits of so many people that all Pennsylvanians can claim him as their own.

"Bensalem is the home of the Smarty Jones," he said. "But as much as I'd like to claim this horse, he belongs to everybody."

SMARTY JONES HAS
EARNED FANS NATIONWIDE
WITH HIS SPEED, BEAUTY
AND CHARISMA.

"I don't see any signs of him starting to tail off."

TRAINER JOHN SERVIS

SMARTY JONES HAS FINAL TUNEUP FOR BELMONT

RICHARD ROSENBLATT

May 29, 2004

BENSALEM, PA.—John Servis can breathe a little easier: Smarty Jones' final tuneup was flawless.

The trainer watched from the backstretch as his Triple Crown threat worked seven furlongs Friday morning at Philadelphia Park—his only timed workout before the Belmont Stakes.

"Absolutely perfect," Servis said. "As far as I'm concerned, we're right on schedule."

With jockey Stewart Elliott aboard, Smarty Jones glided along the track so efficiently his hoofbeats were barely audible as he passed by the grandstand.

Though the time of 1:29.20 was slow, it was the type of work Servis was looking for to keep his Kentucky Derby and Preakness winner content.

"He got to playing a little bit toward the end of his cooling out period, and let out a few squeals," Servis said, "so I may let him get a real strong gallop Tuesday, or something along those lines. I'm real happy where he is right now."

So is Elliott, who rarely works out Smarty.

"He felt super," Elliott said. "He's the same old Smarty Jones."

Of course, there's still a week to go before the Belmont, when Smarty Jones will attempt to become the 12th Triple Crown winner and first since Affirmed in 1978. But to have the final major workout over without incident is a huge relief. Especially since it went so well.

Last year, Funny Cide's final workout before his Triple try was a disaster. The 2003 Derby and Preakness winner blazed five furlongs in 57.80 four days before the Belmont, then finished third in the slop behind Empire Maker.

Servis is well aware of Funny Cide's exploits, as well as what else can occur in the final days before the Belmont.

"I try to think positive, but it's a horse race and a whole lot can go wrong," he said. "I can't tell you how many times I've run the best horses and gotten beat. Look at War Emblem stumbling at the gate. And Funny Cide blew out in 58. There are so many things that can go wrong."

Now that Smarty Jones has cleared a major hurdle, his training schedule tapers off: A walk Saturday, a jog Sunday, a gallop early next week, a van ride to Belmont Park either Tuesday night or Wednesday and a gallop or two over a track he has never run on.

And then it's Belmont time, where racing officials are expecting a record crowd nearing 125,000 to watch Smarty Jones try to end racing's longest drought between Triple Crown winners, 26 years.

If he succeeds, Smarty would join Seattle Slew as the only other horse to win the Triple Crown with an undefeated record, and also become racing's richest thoroughbred with earnings totaling nearly $13 million.

So far, Smarty Jones hasn't shown any signs of fatigue. Since the May 15 Preakness, the smallish, red chestnut has been full of energy and had to be restrained in his gallops before Friday's workout. Trainer Bob Baffert, who watched his three Derby-Preakness winners all come up short in the Belmont, has said the wear and tear on Triple contenders usually begins about two weeks before the Belmont.

Smarty Jones, Servis says, may be getting stronger.

"As good as he came out of the Preakness, I was shocked," Servis said. "And he's showing me signs that he can be going forward. I don't see any signs of him starting to tail off."

PETE VAN TRUMP AND SMARTY JONES MAKE A FINAL PRACTICE RUN BEFORE HEADING TO NEW YORK AND THE BELMONT STAKES.
AP/WWP

AFFIRMED WAS THE LAST TRIPLE CROWN WINNER IN 1978.

Getty Images

SMARTY JONES LOOKS FOR SWEEP, BUT THERE ARE MANY WAYS TO GET TRIPPED UP IN THE BELMONT

RICHARD ROSENBLATT

May 30, 2004

NEW YORK (AP)—The Triple Crown is racing's greatest challenge, so it stands to reason that it takes an exceptional horse to sweep the Kentucky Derby, Preakness and Belmont Stakes.

Greatness now awaits Smarty Jones, who on Saturday will attempt to end 26 years of Triple torment when the undefeated Derby and Preakness winner takes on a handful of rivals in the 1½-mile Belmont, the longest and most grueling race in the series.

Since Affirmed became the 11th Triple Crown champion in 1978, nine 3-year-olds have come tantalizingly close, only to fall short in the Belmont. A safety pin may have derailed Spectacular Bid. Silver Charm was wiped out by fatigue. War Emblem stumbled.

"You need an extra special horse to pull it off, plus you need good fortune, too," says Steve Cauthen, who rode Affirmed to three stirring victories. "But the more Smarty Jones races, the more he's looking like a champion."

The smallish, red chestnut colt has blown away the competition in all eight of his races, and is coming off a record 11½-length romp in the Preakness. And it appears there is no horse capable of stopping Smarty

Jones in the Belmont, also known as "The Test of the Champion."

If he wins, it ends the longest drought between Triple Crown winners. After Citation won it in 1948, a quarter-century passed before Secretariat came through in 1973, topped off by a record-setting 31-length triumph in the Belmont.

Ron Turcotte, who rode Secretariat, boldly proclaimed Smarty can win by 25 lengths. "I feel very confident the horse is being handled just right, and that he's the real thing," he said.

But when it comes to tackling the Belmont, just about anything can happen. So much has gone wrong for so many that there have been 17 near-misses since Sir Barton became the first Triple Crown winner in 1919.

No trainer is more familiar with Triple misfortune than Bob Baffert. Three times since 1997, Baffert had a horse win the Derby and Preakness and fail in the Belmont.

Silver Charm tired in the stretch and was beaten by three-quarters of a length by Touch Gold in '97; Real Quiet fell victim to a poor ride by Kent Desormeaux and lost by a nose to Victory Gallop in '98; and War

"Triple Crown winner Smarty Jones. It rolls right off the tongue, doesn't it?"

FAN QUOTE

Emblem stumbled at the start and finished eighth two years ago.

After the third try, Baffert tried to find humor in defeat: "The next time I win the Derby," he said, "I'm heading home."

Trainer Bud Delp may have entertained similar thoughts in 1979, when Spectacular Bid appeared a cinch to follow Seattle Slew (1977) and Affirmed ('78) as the third consecutive Triple Crown champion. The Bid came into the Belmont with a 12-race winning streak and was an overwhelming 3-10 favorite. He finished third.

Two days after the race, Delp revealed The Bid had stepped on a safety pin in his stall the morning of the race. However, the colt's undoing likely occurred when jockey Ronnie Franklin got caught up in a speed duel with an 85-1 long shot.

There was a frightening end to the '99 Belmont, when Charismatic broke a bone in his left leg approaching the wire but still finished third. Jockey Chris Antley dismounted just past the finish line and cradled the colt's leg, keeping weight off it until veterinarians arrived.

Last year, trainer Barclay Tagg was uneasy throughout the Triple grind with Funny Cide, the popular New York-bred gelding.

Tagg tried to map out a perfect plan to keep Funny Cide fit, but the horse worked out way too fast a few days before the race, and heavy rains on race day turned the track into a sloppy mess. Funny Cide finished third behind Empire Maker, a horse he had beaten soundly in the Derby.

"I don't care how great a horse is going, they will come apart on you a little bit if every little step doesn't go right," Tagg said.

Smarty Jones' final workout went smoothly at Philadelphia Park on Friday, and now trainer John Servis will spend the next week trying to make sure nothing unusual happens.

"I realize now why there has only been a handful of horses to win the Triple Crown," he said. "It's a very grueling road and we've been on it since January."

So far, Smarty Jones has given Servis no reason to believe he won't join Seattle Slew as the only undefeated Triple Crown winners. Servis is confident, yet well aware of the pitfalls.

"I can't tell you how many times I've run the best horses and gotten beat," Servis said. "Look at War Emblem stumbling at the gate. And Funny Cide. There are so many things that can go wrong."

THOUSANDS LAMENT SMARTY JONES' LOSS AT PHILADELPHIA PARK

MIKE GARAFOLO

June 6, 2004

BENSALEM, PA.—Tears of joy turned to tears of sadness within seconds at Philadelphia Park.

Thousands of fans had jammed Smarty Jones' home track on Saturday in hopes of seeing the colt run from his stable on Street Rd. into the history books.

For about two minutes, their wishes had been fulfilled.

As Smarty Jones charged down the stretch, leading the Belmont Stakes by a length, the crowd inside the track's Ultimate Sportsview Bar was already celebrating.

Several fans threw their fists into the air and patted each other on the back. One woman, sitting atop her husband's shoulders, clasped her hands together as her eyes began to well up.

Then, Birdstone began to pass the unpassable horse.

The "Go, Smarty" chants became pleads of "No, Smarty" and the premature celebration instantaneously ceased. Suddenly, the din that began at 9:30 a.m. when the doors opened was lost amid a deafening silence.

Smarty Jones had lost by a length.

"The Philly Jinx rides again," said Jeff Rosenthal, one of a group of five that arrived around 1 p.m. "We should be getting used to this by now." Minutes before post time, Rosenthal had said that "this horse has no idea what he has riding on his back: the hopes and dreams of this city."

Rosenthal wasn't alone. Many fans saw Smarty Jones as an end to Philadelphia's 21-year championship drought. His win over 19 other horses in the Kentucky Derby and his runaway victory in the Preakness Stakes had convinced the crowd they were about to see the first Triple Crown winner since 1978.

About 350 people gathered near the Philadelphia Museum of Art to cheer on the hometown favorite, watching on a large television set up in the middle of the Benjamin Franklin Parkway. The crowd broke out in whoops and hollers as Smarty Jones raced down the track, but grew sullen at the end.

"We thought we had it, because we had no other experience ... he was undefeated," said Joe King, 36, of Philadelphia, a vendor host for the television shopping channel QVC.

Mary Ellen Bennett, a Bensalem mortgage specialist who watched the race on the Parkway, called the loss heartbreaking and "a typical Philadelphia sports story."

At Philadelphia Park, officials did not release an official attendance, but estimates ranged from 15,000 to 20,000. Fans stood shoulder-to-shoulder in the bar, while some sat on steps near TVs. One woman sat with her three children on the floor.

All of them cheered Smarty Jones in the post parade. In fact, the only pre-race boos were for Rock Hard Ten and the song "New York, New York."

When Smarty Jones took the early lead, the crowd stood and cheered. After the race, they sat and second-guessed.

"He broke too soon," one man yelled at the TV screen.

Another bemoaned jockey Stewart Elliot's idle whip at the top of the stretch: "He didn't hit him."

Two younger fans were prepared, however. Jason Burnside and J.S. Hess bet Smarty in a series of exactas —to come in second.

"We didn't want to celebrate," Burnside said after collecting his $139. "Nobody here wanted to hear us cheering."

But there remained others who needed no financial compensation to leave content. They were simply happy to be along for the five-week ride.

"I still love him," Theresa Jones said as she shuffled past a pile of discarded betting slips. "He's still No. 1 in my book."

SMARTY JONES, BIRDSTONE AND THE OTHER
HORSES CHARGE OUT OF THE STARTING GATE AT
THE BELMONT STAKES.

YOUNG FANS VISIT
SMARTY JONES IN HIS
STALL AT BELMONT
PARK.

"There's a lot of Smarty Jones yet to come."

FAN QUOTE

SMARTY JONES STILL PHILLY'S CHAMP DESPITE FAILED TRIPLE CROWN BID

DAN GELSTON

June 6, 2004

BENSALEM, PA.—Just when Philadelphia thought it had a champion it could count on, Smarty Jones failed to bring home horse racing's most coveted prize: the Triple Crown.

Depending on perspective, it was another tale of Philly again choking in the clutch or a horse that had little to prove with Kentucky Derby and Preakness victories already under its saddle.

Trainer John Servis reminded everyone that his only goal five months ago was just qualifying for the Kentucky Derby.

"I'm a Philadelphia sports fan myself," Servis said after the Belmont. "Our championship was the Kentucky Derby. If they can't accept that, they need to take this trip down the Triple Crown one more time and see where I'm coming from."

But it's also easy to see where Philly sports fans are coming from. It's been 21 years since the City of Brotherly Love has won a pro sports championship— the longest drought of any city with four major professional sports teams.

Then along came Smarty Jones, the plucky red chestnut colt that had more than jockey Stewart Elliott on his back. So were the title hopes of Philly fans who have suffered and cried right along with the players through the championship drought.

Taking the first two legs of the Triple Crown gave Philadelphia faith that Smarty Jones could be the first horse to win the elusive Triple Crown in 27 years. There would be a parade and more magazine covers and more hoopla at tiny Philadelphia Park where the hometown team made good.

Instead, Smarty fans from around the area were as blue as Smarty's silks over another championship dream deferred.

Still, fans back at Philly Park on Sunday refused to believe the horse choked under pressure like the Eagles in the last three NFC title games or the Flyers last month in the Eastern Conference finals.

"No!" said Anne Orthner, of Hammonton, N.J. "The Triple Crown is way too elusive. We still have the Breeders' Cup and the Pennsylvania Derby. There's a lot of Smarty Jones yet to come."

Bob Romani, who owns Eagles season tickets and is a partial season-ticket holder for the Phillies, said Smarty's loss was a disappointment but not comparable to the pro sports failures.

"It was just a good story because John Servis and everybody else represented the horse with class and did things the right way," said Romani, of Philadelphia. "It was great that he won the big two. To win the Triple Crown only would have been a bonus."

Some were more crestfallen.

"It's typical Philly luck," said Anthony Siegfried, of Bensalem, which claims to be the true home of Smarty Jones. "We come out with a great horse, Philly wants it and now look what happened. He still won more championships in a month than Philly did the last 10 years. You don't see us booing him."

SMARTY JONES HEADS HOME TO PHILADELPHIA AND WILL GET A
MUCH-DESERVED BREAK BEFORE THE BREEDER'S CUP IN OCTOBER.

AP/WWP

**DIANA OKON SHOWS HER
SUPPORT FOR SMARTY JONES.**
Stan Honda/AFP/Getty Images

Philly fans should rejoice that Smarty could do what Donovan McNabb or Allen Iverson have yet to accomplish—bring home not just one, but two championships.

Still, the fans so badly wanted the third.

Tears of joy turned to tears of sadness within seconds from the thousands of fans who jammed Philadelphia Park on Saturday. At the Belmont, the colt had a rock star-like reception when he peeked out from under a tunnel that led to the paddock area. Those throaty "Go Smarty!" yells were suddenly silenced as Birdstone crossed the finish line first.

There were no Carolina Panthers apologizing for their win in the NFC title game like Birdstone trainer Edgar Prado did after he was booed in the winner's circle.

"I heard when he came back and there were a lot of cheers for him, so that made me feel good," Servis said of Smarty's walk back to the barn. "For the American people, they wanted it so bad. What are you going to do? It's an unfortunate thing."

But rooting for the Flyers and the Eagles is as institutional for Philly sports fans as drinking a Yuengling or devouring a Tastykake. Season tickets and tales of those oh-so-close defeats are passed down for generations.

The collapse of the 1964 Phillies is probably more recalled than their 1980 World Series win.

Fans have only been on the Smarty bandwagon for six weeks. Forget about wait till next year. He could easily be forgotten, just like Funny Cide, whose own bid for a Triple Crown stalled last year at the Belmont and grazed in near anonymity two barns down from Smarty over the weekend.

But it was quite a ride while it lasted for Philadelphia.

"Smarty won our hearts," said Melanie Schreffler, of Southampton, Pennsylvania. "He didn't have to do anything after the Derby."

"We're not done. We've got a lot more things ahead of us." *TRAINER JOHN SERVIS*

SMARTY JONES: HE'LL BE BACK

BETH HARRIS

June 7, 2004

NEW YORK—Smarty Jones is going on vacation. The small chestnut colt who captured the public's fancy has earned a rest after a grueling five-week stretch in which he came up one length short of winning the Triple Crown.

Smarty Jones won the Kentucky Derby and Preakness, but was overtaken in the stretch by 36-1 long shot Birdstone on Saturday in the $1\frac{1}{2}$-mile Belmont Stakes.

Trainer John Servis plans to give Smarty Jones three or four weeks off.

"I'll let him rest up and put him on a schedule for the Breeders' Cup (in October)," Servis said Sunday after getting his first good night's sleep in quite a while.

"We're not done. We've got a lot more things ahead of us."

After the break, Smarty Jones could run in the Pennsylvania Derby at his home track near Philadelphia as a thank you to the local fans. Then there's the Breeders' Cup in Texas.

Owners Pat and Roy Chapman want to run Smarty as a 4-year-old next year.

As expected, Smarty's rivals went after him with a vengeance in the Belmont. They forced him into the lead with a mile to go and pressed the pace so much that the colt was tiring when he hit the top of the stretch.

When jockey Stewart Elliott tried to urge Smarty home to victory, he had already run too fast and Birdstone blew past him.

"Stew was a little upset. He felt he would have settled if those guys hadn't pressed him so hard," Servis said. "He knew they were just sacrificing their horses. He had horses breathing down his neck."

And Servis didn't blame any of the other jockeys for their tactics.

"If you got a horse going for the Triple Crown, he's got a bull's-eye on him. Those people have nothing to lose," he said. "You pull out all the stops."

Winning trainer Nick Zito didn't mind being a bit player in Smarty's big show.

"Smarty Jones was a worthy star," he said. "The average person was there because of Smarty Jones. He has done a lot."

Zito, who won his first Belmont in 12 tries, apologized to Servis after the race. Winning jockey Edgar Prado expressed regret at spoiling Smarty's party, as did Birdstone's owner Marylou Whitney.

"I don't know of anyone who would be more deserving than Nick," Servis said.

The Chapmans plan to tour Kentucky horse farms in the next few weeks in search of a future home for Smarty Jones once his breeding days begin. They want a place that will allow easy access to fans.

"If he had settled, he would have got $1\frac{1}{2}$ miles," Servis said. "You would have had a Triple Crown winner, I guarantee that. In my heart, I feel he was the best horse."

FANS WELCOME HERO SMARTY JONES HOME TO PHILADELPHIA PARK
UPON HIS RETURN FROM BELMONT.
AP/WWP

"*I still love him. He's still No. 1 in my book.*"

SMARTY JONES AND STEWART ELLIOTT HEAD DOWN
THE STRETCH, LEADING BY FOUR LENGTHS.